HEROIC
CAREGIVER

An Anthology Of
Lessons On Resilience,
Coping, And Laughter

PAMELA D. STRAKER, PhD
Caregiver And Editor

INDIE BOOKS
INTERNATIONAL

ISBN-13: 978-1-957651-64-4
Library of Congress Control Number: 2024903065

Designed by Steve Plummer

INDIE BOOKS INTERNATIONAL®, INC.
2511 WOODLANDS WAY
OCEANSIDE, CA 92054
www.indiebooksintl.com

TO MY SISTER:
DR. ALLYSON STRAKER-BANKS

Dear Ally,

As I write this, I am filled with gratitude for the incredible journey we embarked upon together in caring for our beloved mother. Though this path demanded much from us—patience, strength, and sacrifice—it was a journey that spoke to one of our family values, to care for those who came before us. We were so fortunate to provide care in the context of love and respect. Even with those components, it was not an easy road…

From the bottom of my heart, I want to thank you for everything you did during the time of mom's need for care and during this subsequent period of our lives. Your dedication, love, and unwavering support have not only been a pillar of strength for our mother but have also been a source of comfort and inspiration for me.

In these moments, I have seen the best of what it means to be a family. We laughed together, cried together, and above all, supported each other through thick and thin. This experience has, as our parents would have wished, brought to life invaluable lessons about love, resilience, and the importance of family.

We will continue to work hand in hand, sharing our strengths and weaknesses, drawing strength from each other, and from the love that surrounds us. Together, we are a formidable team, and I am proud to stand by your side.

With all my love and gratitude,
Pam

CONTENTS

PREFACE

"How far you go in life depends on your being tender with the young, compassionate with the aged, sympathetic with the striving, and tolerant of the weak and strong. Because someday in your life you will have been all of these." –George Washington Carver

I T HAS BEEN an honor to capture the stories recounted by those who have contributed to this book, which is filled with stories told by caregivers: people who find themselves taking care of their loved ones and dealing with age-related illnesses and other health problems. Some are my own stories; some are those of friends. Also, I reached beyond my family and friends to collect stories via a Reddit post. As AARP 2020 statistics indicate, most of those I had the privilege of speaking with are related to the party for whom they are providing care.

The stories are organized thematically. You will see that some may fall under more than one thematic category. That is how life is. Experiences and stories do not necessarily fit neatly into one category.

Each story was chosen to show a variety of caregiver experiences that are common to those caring for their parents or for other persons they love. There is sadness in some of the stories but also a lot of goodwill and humor, which are often the keys to getting through the day and the situations that occur. Stories were chosen as the format for this book to enable a more personal way of communicating caregivers' experiences.

Since life happens day by day, these stories are meant to be snapshots into the scenarios caregivers encounter on a regular basis. Some may be familiar to you, others you can identify with or perhaps have heard about something similar from a friend or colleague.

This book, not meant to be a textbook, is written

to give caregivers a voice and a context in which they can appreciate themselves, the many complexities they manage, and their right and responsibility to seek happiness even when caring for others. Further, the book is meant to offer an opportunity for caregivers to explore and redefine how they perceive themselves and how they are perceived by others. While this is not a "how to" book, it opens the door to discussion about some of the issues caregiving brings to the foreground.

As you read, please feel free to skip around, to make the experience yours.

DR. PAMELA STRAKER
NEW YORK CITY

WELCOME, CAREGIVER

"It's not the load that breaks you down, it's the way you carry it." –**Lena Horne**

BEING A CAREGIVER is a noble work. Wherever you are on this journey, I salute you, fellow traveler.

While this is not meant to be a traditional "how to" book, my caregiving experiences and those of many of the caregivers with whom I have spoken led me to conceptualize four pivotal heroic caregiving points experienced by caregivers as they begin the journey with those they care for:

1. Call to become a caregiver (recognizing help is needed)

2. Emotional reaction (What do you feel?)

3. Developing the caregiving plan
   (including self-care/resource review)

4. Implementation

CALL TO BECOME A CAREGIVER

When you look back on how the caregiving phase begins, it's often the beginning of a series of vignettes: The stove gas is left on, the driving deteriorates, there's less conversation. Tasks that were previously accomplished without difficulty become laborious or impossible for our loved ones to accomplish. Sometimes you see it but at first you don't focus until perhaps there is an outstanding event that cannot be ignored. You may come to realize your loved one is in real danger.

YOUR EMOTIONAL REACTION

In recognition of the required change in the role of the observer of the vignettes—moving from "observer" to "caregiver"—many feelings may be experienced. The feeling of being overwhelmed or numbed may be felt, though not necessarily expressed, as the first emotion. Following this, various feelings may appear as the new role and its requirements emerge: anger, loss, fear, sadness, joy, and more.

DEVELOPING THE PLANS

The plan for the one who currently requires care may be extensive or less so, depending upon what was previously put in place. Developing a plan for the current caregiver (I call it a Caregiver Legacy Plan) should be considered a priority. Regardless of what the focus of the plan is (person receiving care or caregiver), the caregiver's need for self-care should be included. Are your medical numbers in order? Do you need therapy/counseling? What are the resources available to provide the care needed? Are you the only person who can do so? Are there siblings or other family members who should be included? Do financial resources exist? Are they readily accessible? Are there agencies or organizations that can help? Is the plan written?

IMPLEMENTATION

Is the person for whom you are providing care capable of being part of the implementation? Are they able to state any realistic preferences they may have? What if aspects of the plan don't work? What is the timeline for implementing the plan?

SPECIAL CONSIDERATIONS
FOR HEROIC CAREGIVERS

The following can be applied to many of the stories in this book. Think about how they apply as you read the stories and/or as you consider your caregiving journey. Consider:

Creativity is required in caregiving. Many times our solutions are found in the moment. Caregivers are often concerned they don't know how to handle every situation. The truth is, even the best, most experienced caregivers will be stumped from time to time regarding the solution to a problem.

Laughter helps. Finding humor in what can become little trying circumstances is required for caregiving, as this wariness is likely to continue for some period of time in the elderly. When humor no longer softens a particular situation, patience and attention to detail are needed.

Be prepared. Being prepared means watching over your loved one during a hospital stay. Even in the best of circumstances, mistakes happen. Caregiving requires vigilance while a loved one is in the hospital so something disastrous doesn't take place.

It's a family affair. Sometimes other family members do not have the ability to make a plan and implement it as well as our heroic caregivers. Implementation often requires the caregiver to be in good health, live in the same general area, and have the time and/or the resources to offer to the full-time task of caregiving. Things become much more difficult when the caregiver has health issues.

Distractions happen. Even with the most focused caregivers, it is possible to be distracted or stressed by responsibilities for those we care for. Caregivers need to balance caring for their loved ones with making certain they care for themselves. Sometimes, this is not such an easy task.

Morale matters. The level of required care and the duration of it can negatively affect a caregiver's morale. Fortunately, some loved ones live a long life before they need extensive care even though providing care is never easy in the short or long term.

Solutions will appear. As long as we operate from a place of love and peace, we will find an appropriate solution, in time. Meditating, praying, screaming, and begging may take place first, but in the end there is always a way to fix a problem.

Some caregiving is easier to work through than others. Sometimes, the more mobile and lucid your loved one being cared for is, the more difficult it can be to work through problems. Your loved one may fear losing their sense of independence.

1

DANGER

"If you don't like something, change it. If you can't change it, change your attitude." **–Maya Angelou**

IT JUST HAD TO BE DONE

AFTER TAKING CARE of her husband for thirteen years without help before his demise, my mom was an energetic, in-charge, "I-can-do-it" kind of person who had begun to have strokes. Her doctors shared with us that she had to be watched because of her tendency to be somewhat impulsive. But she was still taking care of herself fully so this was not taken as seriously as it might have been if she had not been able to care for herself.

One day, my brother arrived at Mom's house.

He entered and walked through the immaculately cared-for home and found our mother in the dining room. The light from the sparkling clean windows fell beautifully upon the shiny, polished dining room table. The candlesticks on the table came into view as did Mom standing on top of the shiny dining room table with a dust cloth in hand.

Her son gasped and managed to ask, "What are you doing?" to which she matter-of-factly stated, "I am cleaning the chandelier of course. It just had to be done!"

Still a little in shock at the sight, my brother replied, "Well, I am just not sure we want to visit the emergency room or the steps to the pearly gates today, Mom." She reluctantly accepted help down from the table.

BABUSHKA

I arrived home on a snowy day. It was dark and at least four inches of snow was on the ground. As I pulled into the driveway, I observed my mother shoveling, wearing a long coat and what can only be described as a babushka—a lightweight headscarf tied below the chin—on her head. I simply said, "I don't think this

is a good idea," and headed toward the door of the house, knowing that would surprise her. Her expectation would be that I would either take the shovel away and begin shoveling or join her in shoveling. The other option was arguing about the shoveling. My mother came into the house within three minutes.

THE CASE OF THE DISAPPEARING DAD OR *L'AMOUR À DEUX*

L'amour à deux is French for "a love shared by two."

When I arrived on the back step (which housed two doorways, one to my mom's home and one to mine) at 9:30 p.m., my mother was outside. "Your father hasn't come home," she exclaimed.

I asked, "When did you see him last?"

Her response was, "This morning before I went to the hairdresser at 10:30; when I returned at 2:30 he was gone."

I was stunned. "Why didn't you call me at work?" There was no response. The car was gone so my father had driven somewhere.

I went to my mother's house. I called my sister, who lived one-and-a-half hours away. She organized the cavalry; my brother-in-law was on his way. I called my aunt (father's sister) and uncle who lived two hours away—they had not seen him. I had no alternative other than calling the local police precinct.

Several police officers descended upon the house. They searched every room and every closet on every floor. They seemed more nosey than interested in whether my father was stowed away anywhere in the house. What was remarkable about this was my mother's cheerful and helpful stance; she was normally a person who was concerned about "strangers" coming into her home. In this instance, she was leading them through the house with no hesitation.

I sat down, considering what to do next. At about 11:00 p.m., I heard the kitchen door open and my father came in. He was his usual cheerful self. He was dressed in the expensive casual clothing my mother always purchased for him, wool gabardine pants and a silk bomber jacket. On his wrist was a gold ID bracelet encrusted with his initials in diamonds.

I calmed myself and asked, "Dad, where have you been?"

"Oh, I went for a ride," he answered casually.

I pushed on. "May I see your wallet?"

My father pulled his wallet out of one pocket. In it were four crisp one hundred dollar bills. Well, at least he wasn't robbed.

"May I see what's in your other pocket?" My father pulled out an invoice from a store two hours away. So my dad had driven on a highway and returned, during a time when there were construction points on the highway that required deviating from the normal course. The drive under normal circumstances was two hours and fifteen minutes long each way. I called a friend who confirmed my father had visited and had dinner there. I called my sister and brother-in-law to have them cancel their trip here.

My mother and father sat on the couch in their living room. My mother, so happy to see my dad, said, "You see, your father always says things will work out." They seemed totally oblivious to the dangers my dad had escaped.

I left them, tears streaming down my face.

SHE WENT TOO FAR

It was the holiday season of 2007 after one of my mom's strokes from which she appeared to have fully recovered. My mother loved the holiday season—music performed with a full orchestra, the eight-foot tree at her home, gift shopping, giving to charities, the family gathering, and so much more.

I went to her home late in the day to find her absent. She arrived home, all five feet, three and a half inches of her, with her handbag slung across her body and an additional shopping bag. Where had she been? My mother reported that she had been at a huge intersection handing out holiday cards. Picture it: a petite woman in her mid-seventies, alone, with a pocketbook and no cell phone, at a location where five roads intersected, three train stops emptied, and the sidewalks were filled with hundreds of people.

I was practically speechless but I managed to say, "You've tested this out once and you were somehow protected. Please don't try it again." Thankfully, she never did.

ONLY THE DOCTOR HAD THE POWER

Dad was always the driver for the family. Mom had always embraced her role as passenger, seeing driving as the male role. We started to hear about little bumper-denting incidents, so we began to ride with Dad on a monthly basis to observe how his driving was going. Unfortunately, it had become hesitant and extremely slowed.

We begged Mom to stop having Dad drive and assume possession of the keys. She refused, indicating this would negatively affect Dad's self-esteem. Finally, after yet another small "bumper" incident, we called the doctor Dad and Mom visited on a monthly basis. At their next visit, while discussing Dad's driving, the doctor came from behind the desk, sat next to Mom, and asked, "Mrs. C., do you want to die in the car with your husband?" Mom drove Dad home from the doctor and Dad did not drive again.

THE SPIDERS DID IT!

I am not sure if this was done before, but I thought maybe we all would like to start the week off with a giggle or two to get through the day.

Both my father and my mom had dementia. They were seeing things that weren't there or happening all the time. He kept seeing spiders coming out of the recessed lighting in their home. He said they crawled out and then grew to be six feet wide and tall. These spiders would climb on top of him and try to eat him but he would hide under the blanket. This went on for a while. One day he told me he took a ring box and covered the six-foot-wide spider for me to see.

One night he called me again and said, "The spiders, the spiders," and hung up. I went flying over to find my dad and my mom standing under the fan/light spraying a can of foot fungus spray and a can of Pam cooking spray to kill them. The whole ceiling was soaked. They both told me the spiders asked daddy to give them a bath, so he did.

Every time I see a spider, I think of that night and have to laugh.

That night I moved in with them and was there until their passing.

A LITTLE BACKGROUND

Our remarkable mom is now 103, and God-willing will reach 104 in October. A caregiver for much of her life, Mom had an extraordinary career while being an even more extraordinary wife, mother, aunt, grandmother, great-grandmother, and friend. She has been my inspiration and has affected the lives of countless others in her roles as social worker, counselor, mental health coordinator, and social services director. My sisters and I have always said it takes four of us to make one of her.

Mom, my husband, and I live in a three-story home with *her* cat, Blue. Both my husband and I work full-time. The blessing within my caregiver's experience is that I have help. My devoted, phenomenal first cousin spends weekdays with Mom, caring for her until I return from work. My phenomenal, devoted three sisters pitch in and help when they can, and my dear, darling, and amazing husband provides respite for me as well. I could not do it without them. Despite their support, I have to say being the primary caretaker is not for the faint of heart.

Wow. I have dozens of little stories to relate, some poignant, some sweet, some funny, some utterly frustrating and sad—all bittersweet. Let's see.

A SCARY NIGHT: THE NIGHT MOM WOKE UP AT 3:00 A.M. TO GO TO THE LOO

Several years ago, Mom was fully mobile, able to navigate all the stairs, and still sleeping in her bedroom on the second floor. On this particular evening, while sleeping soundly on the third floor, I heard—almost felt—a loud thud. Mom's groans snapped me out of my slumber. I leaped out of bed and ran downstairs, dreading what I would find.

Mom had walked down the long hall, in the dark, stumbled past the commode, and mistaken the tub for the toilet. In her sleepy state, she tried to sit down and fell backward in the bathtub, hitting her knee, head, and back. When I turned on the light and found her in the tub, I jumped nearly five feet to reach her. There was no blood. Thank God. She was conscious. Thank heaven. She was moaning. Not good but understandable. There was nothing broken I could see. Praise the Lord. Somehow, together, we found the strength to get her up on her feet and out of the tub.

What followed was a whirlwind of activity: I gave her water and four low-dose aspirins; put a cold, wet towel around her head; wrapped an ace bandage around her knee; checked her all over; and helped her down the hallway and back into bed. She seemed okay and relieved to be back in her room, in her bed. *Was I doing the right thing? Should I have called 911? Will she be okay the rest of the night?* Next, a fitful sleep—at least for me.

In the morning, I woke up early and called her doctor, who advised me to get her to a specialist. I found an orthopedic surgeon and got a same-day appointment. Getting from the house to the car was an adventure in itself. There are thirteen stairs from the second to the first floor, and another twenty-one stairs and a significant walkway from the porch to the street. Using a cane and leaning on my arm, Mom navigated the stairs slowly, eventually reaching the sidewalk. I had to leave her on her own, bracing against a tree, trusting she could hold herself together until I returned with the car. Mom managed to get in and out of the car, and once at the doctor's office was able to walk fairly well. The doctor diagnosed a torn meniscus, prescribed pain meds, and gave her a few options—the last of which was to do nothing. Mom liked the last option, continued to use a cane for a while, and toughed it out without surgery.

A SCARY MORNING: THE TIME I CAUGHT MOM AS SHE FELL

This happened a number of years ago. For some reason—Providence? Divine intervention?—I woke up earlier than usual and went downstairs before 6:00 a.m. Walking along the first-floor hallway, I glimpsed Mom in the den and shouted good morning to her. She didn't respond in kind but instead said she didn't feel well and began to stagger. I ran to help and just as I reached her, she fell into my arms and we began falling. Amazingly—some would say by the grace of God—we landed in the recliner in a twisted embrace.

Mom had a terrible headache, was nauseous, and felt like she would throw up. *Heart attack? Stroke?* I wriggled away and raced to get aspirin and water, which she was able to swallow. Then I helped her to the bathroom. *But what next? Do I call 911? Oh no, where's my cell phone?* Watching Mom like a hawk, I could see she was improving. Moments later, she was much better. *Was the emergency over?* I figured I had time to run upstairs and get my cell phone.

Okay, now what? Is it time to call 911? Do I just make the call? This is where the mother-daughter relationship gets tricky, and mother eclipses daughter. I actually asked my mom if she wanted me to call 911. Mom's response: *No! I can't go to the hospital like this. Get my lipstick and earrings. I have to do my hair and get dressed. Iron my white blouse. Call your sisters.* Mom was rational, in command, and definitely herself.

Being an obedient daughter, I called my sisters and cousin, two of whom got to the house in record time. By then, Mom was fully back to herself. Since the crisis had passed, I was given the okay to go to choir rehearsal—one of my great joys. Once Mom was dressed (to her satisfaction) the call was made to 911. The girls had rallied. (Funny how we're in our seventies but still "the girls.") Mom was admitted to the hospital, placed on new meds, and released a few days later.

2

CHANGING ROLES

"Yes we can!" –Barack Obama

THE SIGNS ARE THERE

ARRIVED AT MY parents' home and noted that the garage door was open. I checked further and when the sensor light came on, I noticed that the snowblower was gone. It clearly was not in use since it was spring and there was no snow in sight.

When I went into the house, bags of groceries were everywhere, the contents not yet placed in their proper locations. It appeared that my mom had struggled to get my dad inside. His ambulation difficulties sometimes slowed the process.

My mom was making tea for herself and Dad. I admired her "life goes on, get it done" attitude. She was the rock with respect to my dad and she kept everything together.

She refused help of all kinds. Though I had to tell her about the garage and the snowblower, it felt as if I was deflating her to do so. I finished by quickly saying, "I will order a new snowblower tomorrow." I reflected upon the fact that Mom and Dad would need more help as time went on. And so another aspect of the caregiving began.

THE JOURNEY BEGINS

She spent many years caring for her husband, most of the time, without her children's help. A year after his death, her children took her away for the weekend. Everyone was having a great time. Suddenly, her children noticed her eyes were not aligned. They knew they had to get her medical care but they also knew it was difficult to get ambulance service.

They calmly explained to her what was happening and told her of the need to head to the hospital, thirty minutes away, immediately. She resisted a little. They patiently listened to her objections as they guided her to the door.

They pointed the car in the direction of the hospital and began speeding. Along the way, they saw a police car, pulled over, explained the situation, and obtained a police escort to the hospital. At the hospital, an evaluation was done and preliminary treatment was begun but the doctors concluded she needed a higher level of care available at a hospital one and a half hours away.

The children piled into the car and followed the ambulance in a rainstorm. Visibility was enhanced only by the rear lights of the ambulance. The trip took two hours because of the weather. The doctors at the hospital evaluated her and treated her.

They advised that the diagnosis was likely a stroke but further testing would be required. The children were now exhausted. Eighteen hours earlier they had left home; they were directed to a nearby hotel, where sleep was fitful.

They woke up early, ate a light breakfast, and returned to the hospital. A stroke was confirmed. The children visited her and had a conference with the doctors. They drove the three and a half hours home and designed a plan.

They would alternate days of visitation. They contacted her physician and informed him of the situation. In response to their questions about what they should do in an emergency once she returned home, the physician remarked, "I don't do emergencies." This physician was never consulted again. Seventeen years have passed and three additional strokes have happened since they heard that insensitive statement. Many wonderful doctors have assisted the family in getting the best care possible.

In this case, the family had time to plan and manage the implementation of their loved one's long-term care. Sometimes things happen without warning or reason and throw off the best short-term plans.

IT WAS NEVER TOO EARLY!

At 6:00 a.m., I heard shovels at work outside. The forecast had been for a snowstorm with high winds and icing. My heart raced as I went to the window and observed my parents shoveling snow. I went outside and managed to remove the shovel from each of them. Thankfully, I flagged down a group that was shoveling for a fee. Later, I contacted a neighbor, who graciously came over to shovel whenever it snowed.

THE MISCHIEVOUS ONE

Over time, Mom had four strokes and was required to have twenty-four-hour care. She had aphasia, which limited her speaking. She could speak, but not in the long, articulate manner she used to. Her caregivers always commented on the fact that, at almost ninety years old, she heard everything and was not "out of it." My mother maintained her sense of humor and continued to be mischievous, as she had been her entire life.

When she went to the restroom in her home, she had to be accompanied because of her poor ambulation. She had been told this multiple times. What she had begun to do was an expression of her deep sense of independence and her extraordinary will.

Her caregivers would say, "I am going to be downstairs preparing your meal for a bit. Do you need to use the restroom?"

"No, I'm fine," she would reply. Within ten minutes of the caregiver's absence, they could hear her walker moving across the floor and had to return to accompany her.

One day, the caregiver informed Mom that she was going to the store and would return in an hour. She inquired about the restroom. As always, my Mom denied the need for the visit. Fifteen minutes later I arrived, and Mom was at the sink in the restroom. I gave the usual speech about safety, though it was the truncated version.

After she was finished, I helped her sit in her walker and rolled her to the bedroom. When she got to her bed, she suddenly complained it was too hard to stand up and said I would have to help her. I said, "Of course I will help you but I wonder why help is needed now *after* you managed to walk to the restroom alone?" Mom could not help it; she laughed as she realized she was caught "playing the victim" to engage her daughter's full attention and assistance, one of her favorite things to do.

SHE KNEW

Mom had successfully lived on her own until she had a stroke at ninety years old, which was followed by a month of rehab at a skilled nursing facility, when she was diagnosed with vascular dementia. I moved in with Mom and served as her primary caregiver until she passed four years later. One thing I learned was that Mom, even though no longer able to remember things or engage in sustained conversation, clearly still knew how she felt about things. This was true and important for everyone, even the youngest child, to understand that she had clear preferences to be respected.

Mom looked to be greeting her impending death in the same practical, matter-of-fact manner in which she had lived life, seeming to feel at peace. She felt strongly about wanting to donate her body to St. Louis University School of Medicine. She believed the body she would no longer need could still be of some good use to others after her death. Mom always was a big believer in not letting things go to waste.

A lifelong devout Catholic, Mom seemed near the end to feel "right with God" and simply accepted she would be leaving this existence to be reunited with those who had passed before her. She expressed her feelings that her usual practices for honoring God of going to Mass, spiritual reading, meeting with friends from church for a "centering" prayer and spiritual practices group, and receiving communion in the home were no longer needed as she approached the end. She seemed at peace with that decision.

Before her stroke and dementia, Mom had been an avid reader and appreciator of the arts. Once she was no longer able to read, she continued to express a need (in between progressively increased napping) for something to keep her interest (and focus on something); Mom wanted the TV on CNN every day almost all day long. No longer able to remember for long what she had just seen, it was a blessing that Mom was able to enjoy seeing the same newscasts over and over!

Dementia also did not prevent Mom from having developed a surprisingly new preference toward the end of her life; she found it absolutely hilarious to see a seemingly endless procession of people "wipe out" in feats that did not go as planned on *America's Funniest Home Videos*, a TV show she normally would have found to be lowbrow, boring, and not funny. New joys can sometimes come to us even as we are in the process of saying goodbye to this world.

THE ALBATROSS DIED FROM A DOSE OF REALITY

An albatross flying around a ship in the middle of the ocean was an omen of wind, storms, and bad weather to come. It was also considered very unlucky to kill it because sailors believed that the souls of deceased sailors inhabited the albatross. The expression "an albatross around my neck" alludes to the poem "The Rime of the Ancient Mariner" by Samuel Taylor Coleridge.

"Family etiquette" can often feel like an albatross around your neck.

The year was 2009 and my mom was hospitalized due to a stroke. As my sister and I gathered ourselves in the emergency room, we made a list of follow-ups that were needed. We had to assure that Mom's sister was informed. We asked a cousin, who called us during the time we were in the hospital, to call our aunt (also the cousin's aunt).

The next day, the aunt in question called me to inquire why the call had not come directly from me or my sister. The call did not continue on a positive note, and I precipitously ended it, stating, "This is a stressful time and is not the time to harass me or my sister on what you consider to be proper etiquette!"

Several days later, I was at work and received a call from my aunt's son. It was clear this was not going to be a fun call. I gathered myself and my phone and went outside. My cousin complained about my interface with his mother, indicating I damaged the relationship with her.

I paused and at that moment I recalled all the times my nuclear family and I had coped with the negativity coming from this direction. (Oh my goodness—the albatross.) I finally replied, "You know what, I do not have a relationship with your mother and really never have had one. I do not hear from her from one year to the next and when, out of respect for the fact that she is my mother's sister, I ensured she was kept informed, she then called to berate me."

When the call ended, I felt lighter and with a sense of freedom. I had ridden myself of another "family albatross." Bright sunshine emerged as I reentered my workplace. Although my aunt was not always a cheery soul, my mother was happy and outgoing almost to a fault, as seen next.

THE SQUIRREL WAGED THE BATTLES–MOM WON THE WAR

One day we heard noises coming from the air conditioner in the living room. When we looked out, a squirrel was nestled next to the air conditioner, which was installed with plexiglass on either side to maximize the amount of light we received. Further examination revealed the squirrel had eaten into the wood that was the frame of the window.

The squirrel returned every day and could not be chased away. It moved all deterrents, including spikes that were placed in the window's corners. Having paid several hundred dollars in the past to have squirrels trapped and removed only to see them return or be replaced, we were hard-pressed to try that intervention again.

One day, Mom said, "I wish we couldn't see the squirrel." The next day our handyman arrived and painted the plexiglass. The squirrel was still there but we never saw it again.

HAPPY EVENINGS: VISITING THE ACUPUNCTURIST AND TOPS DINER

For a couple of years before the COVID-19 pandemic, Mom, my husband, and I made biweekly trips to an acupuncturist. After these sessions, Mom always walked taller, had more energy, and looked younger. She'd chat up the acupuncturist and regale her with all kinds of stories about her life. Then we three would enjoy a late dinner at Tops, in our opinion New Jersey's best and busiest diner.

Mom developed and exhibited what I'll call a queenly strut, moving slowly among the patrons and drawing them into conversation. Whenever we shared that she was one hundred, people would look at her in utter amazement, ask about her secret, beg for a hug, take a picture, and offer all kinds of compliments—and she would just shine. Another thing she would do—much to our chagrin—was comment on the astonishing sights she saw, just a little too loudly. Fortunately, the music and noise level were always high, the targets never overheard her remarks.

One night, an unusually large woman, with jiggling flesh, lots of makeup, a tight, extravagant outfit, a short skirt, and high heels, tipped by our booth. Not only did Mom roll her eyes and laugh, but she also turned to watch the woman move down the aisle. While doing this, Mom blurted out, "Oh my lord. Do you see her bottom? It is huge!" My husband and I cringed and tried to quiet her. Mom, of course, ignored us and had a good old time, enjoying the people, the place, the food, and talking about whatever and whomever she pleased. As my husband always said, she is one hundred and unfiltered.

A STORY WITHIN THIS STORY
ABOUT CRASHING A FUNERAL

Sometimes, to distract Mom, I would ask her to *tell us about the time*—invariably a funny story from her youth. One of the best was when she crashed a funeral. As a teenager, Mom boarded with Mrs. Anthony while her parents worked out of state. Mrs. Anthony lived next to a church and

Mom would often look out the window and watch funeral processions. On this particular day, Mom was alone and a bit bored. Something about this funeral fascinated her, so she decided to go downstairs and enter the church. It just so happened that when she walked in, she inadvertently joined the end of the family procession. Then she was seated next to an older gentleman who was crying softly. His grief touched her deeply, and she began crying, also softly. When his crying turned to sobs, Mom found herself sobbing with him. One of the church matrons gave Mom a tissue and tried to console her, asking her which of her relatives had died. That question shocked Mom back into her senses; she suddenly realized she had no business being at a stranger's funeral and sitting with the family. She jumped to her feet and ran out of the church.

MEANWHILE, BACK AT TOPS DINER

Mom's appetite was wonderful. After finishing half of her meal (none of us could eat it all), typically Mom would order vanilla ice cream while continuing to enjoy the sights and sounds, talking to anyone and everyone near us. Exiting was always a journey. Imagine her stopping at each table, smiling and striking up a conversation. What would take most patrons an hour-plus took us a minimum of two. We usually got home around midnight. Visiting the acupuncturist and dining out late was our routine until COVID-19 changed the landscape.

TOO MANY SLEEPLESS NIGHTS

Mom had an issue with sleeping most of her adult life. In fact, she was hospitalized in 1978 after going several days without sleep. By the fifth day, her eyes were red and she found herself crying without knowing why. At the time, she was director of social services at a private hospital. Her colleagues knew something was wrong and called a doctor on her behalf. She was admitted and given IV medication, essentially to knock her out.

Forty-four years had passed since then but sleepless nights were still a problem. She resists taking anything to help her sleep but will pray and talk away the hours. While she gets some sleep, it is certainly not enough.

We have tried it all: prescription medication, which Mom takes once and then rejects; OTC meds, which she'll usually try once and refuse to take again, e.g., melatonin in all its varieties—capsules, tabs, gummies; herbal sleep aids; warm milk and honey; warm milk with honey and scotch; and CBD oil, roll-on, and chewable doses.

A few nights ago, we had a serious tête-à-tête about her resistance to taking anything that might help her sleep. It ended with me saying, "I'm done talking. Let's move on." At bedtime, she asked for melatonin and took it. I was amazed. The melatonin took the edge off and she's been a bit nicer, less troubled, more like herself. What's amazing is that she's been agreeing to take it. Hallelujah! Let's hope this continues!

DO AS I SAY

Lately, Mom can become unhinged if we don't do exactly what she says, when she says it. Usually the *cat*alyst is Blue, Mom's Russian blue feral cat. Blue was gifted to us by our youngest sister, our chief cat-lover and owner, when he was around three. Also dubbed His Majesty, Blue spent his first years in a sanitation warehouse in Brooklyn. He thinks he is a person, as does Mom—and not only a person, but also "the alpha dog," if a cat can qualify for that title. On Mom's command, we have to open the door, change his water, let him in, give him fresh food, change his dish, brush off his pillow, take him to the vet, let him out, check his sleeping area, open the door again, keep it open in case he wants to come in, etc. Sometimes I get irritated about being at the cat's beck and call, and then I feel guilty about being irritated. After all, he's my mom's darling pet. The truth is, neither my husband nor I like cats. Compounding this is my recent allergy testing, which revealed my one and only allergic response was to—cats! Say it isn't so! My caregiving has been stretched to include a four-legged creature for whom I have no love, from whom I have allergies, and with whom I live. I am at my best when Blue is out of the house, roaming the neighborhood. Uh oh—Mom is telling me to open the door for Blue. I did. He was not there.

We've experienced plenty of random *do as I say* moments. Out of nowhere, Mom might say, "Don't drink the water. It's bad. I'm the mother. Now, do as I say!" We've learned to agree and keep it moving.

ACCUSATIONS AND EXPLOSIONS

One of my greatest challenges has been to learn not to react to the wildly crazy or hurtful things Mom might say. She often thinks people are in the house, going through her things in her room upstairs, usually sewing and stitching labels on her clothing or washcloths and towels. It's best to ignore her comments, change the subject, offer her something to drink, and talk about the great-grandkids and show her a picture of one of them.

It's taken time and prayer but I'm doing better at not getting angry when she gets accusatory. But it is tough, especially when she attacks my husband, MG, for no good reason. Every now and then, she blames him for the pain that plagues her, which she claims has ruined her life. Because her pain feels like it's electrical, she believes in her heart my husband can fix it and he chooses *not* to. When she goes on a rant, the slings and arrows she spews are terribly upsetting. Most of the time I'm able to take it, walk away, ignore it, or understand it. Once, however, I simply could not take it anymore and *exploded*. I have to pause and share that I've been described as sweet, patient, compassionate, loving, wonderful, and empathetic. It has been said that I'm a saint. Of course, I am not, but you get the idea. For me to explode is a big deal.

On the day in question, Mom hit all my buttons. I don't recall exactly what she said or how long she was ranting. I do know she said a bunch of things about my husband giving people keys to the house, hiring people to kill her, and controlling folks on the street who watch the house and beep their horns. For what seemed like hours I was able to deal with it, not engaging, walking away to calm myself, changing the subject. I was fully aware I was doing well *until* Mom said something about me taking her money. That was when *I totally lost it.* "How can you say such a thing? I have sacrificed my life for you! I have spent the last ten years caring for you. I have been completely devoted to your welfare. Everything MG and I do is for your benefit. How in the world can you say such awful things? How, how, how?" My voice got louder and louder until I was shrieking like a wild banshee and crying hysterically. At the same time, I was banging my right hand on the kitchen table with such force that I broke blood vessels in it. It seemed like an out-of-body experience because I could see and hear myself going absolutely nuts. *Who was this person? Certainly not me.* My husband came running downstairs, lifted me in his arms, and carried me to the living room. He told me in a calm, firm voice to go upstairs and settle down. I did. The rest of the evening was quiet. I thought about staying upstairs, watching TV, and not cooking dinner, but I got myself together, knowing I had to do the right thing. After a couple of hours, I returned to the scene of the explosion and prepared our meal in silence. We also ate in silence. When I got Mom into bed, she apologized, which brought me to tears. I apologized too. The next few days were lovely.

THE CREATIVE GENIUS EMERGES

Besides family and friends, Mom's chief interests are genealogy, creative writing, sketching, and catching up on the news of the day. We use the word "amazing" to describe her, because, well, she is! For much of her adult life, she has been writing poems—personal, reflective, cerebral, and political—and recently has been focusing on children's stories that are so entertaining and clever that we think she missed one of her callings.

Mom has always had an unusual appreciation for, if not a love of animals and creatures, if you consider a bug a creature. One of her latest poems is "Inchworm," inspired by her childhood summers in Media, Pennsylvania. (Media is located in Quaker territory and provided a safe haven for the formerly enslaved. Mom's great-grandparents settled there and married in the Honeycomb UAME Church, an Underground Railroad stop.) In any case, on a typical summer day, young Mom would sit under one of the backyard trees and spend hours absorbed in nature, watching birds, playing with worms, and noticing the peculiar way in which inchworms move.

She's often inspired by programs on TV. Case in point: Mom and a bunch of us watched a documentary called *My Octopus Teacher*. We were all transfixed. Mom was touched to tears, and inspired enough to write a children's story, *The Mischievous Octopus*. Weedie, the protagonist, is a very little octopus with an extra tentacle who loves to tickle his friends, roll up in a ball, and hide. She spent days writing, rewriting, starting all over, getting writer's block, finding inspiration, writing in a different composition notebook, and finally stopping with several versions ready for her "editor."

When Mom is working on a piece, she is laser focused, spending hours at the kitchen table with pencils, paper, composition notebooks, erasers, and a pencil sharpener surrounding her. It is really something to see. My role has been to offer feedback, type everything up, maybe edit a bit, illustrate with online clip art or photos, and print everything in booklets. This creative partnership has given us lots of joy and some hilarious moments.

The downside of this whole process is that she sometimes thinks people are coming into the house and altering what she's written ("I didn't write that! This is terrible! I would never do such a poor job!"), removing pages ("They took my best work and replaced it with this?"), stealing her composition notebooks ("I had another book. Now it's gone! Why is this happening to me—after all the work I've done! I'm not a bad person. Why are they doing this to me?"). In the midst of her rants I have had moments of victory. Whether complaining about ants, water under the floorboards, people coming in the house, and men zapping her with electrical charges, I've been more able to deflect—interrupting her with, "Mom, let's talk about something else. How about your latest story; you're almost done." Sometimes this stops the madness and entirely changes her mood—and she's ready to write!

I am grateful to be able to witness *and* participate in her creative process. When Mom sees the finished product, she is typically overjoyed, appreciative, and motivated to start or revisit a poem or story. It's pretty wonderful.

SHORT STORIES

My mom was very fond of my husband, Paul, and was thanking him for something he did for her. She told him how terrific she thought he was and then turned to me and asked, "How long are you going to let this one stick around?"

My mom was thanking me for being patient when she needed some special help. She said she appreciated it because my aunt had not been so patient with my grandmother, who she took care of for many years. I said, "Well, try me in ten years."

She started to laugh and said, "Oh, you think you are going to be that way too in ten years?"

Toward the end my mom had a moment of clarity and said, "You know, you are taking care of me. What would I do if you were not here?"

I said, "Just think about it, Mom; you would be with (my brother) Richard!" We both started to laugh because he did not have the right temperament for caregiving.

My mom had trouble distinguishing between dreams and reality toward the end. It was Thanksgiving dinner and she refused to eat anything and was very quiet until after dinner and we were putting food away. Then she called my older son over and said, "Don't ask any questions, just run out to the cart outside; the food is poisoned." I explained she was just having a dream and everything was fine. Then she asked to eat and proceeded to eat a full plate of food. She laughed when I pointed out that she didn't prevent any of us from eating if she thought it was poisoned.

We had a little gap in time when my mom's caregivers could not be with her, so I was covering for them. I jokingly asked her to be easy on me since I really did not know what I was doing. She said, with her favorite caregiver there, also jokingly, "That's okay; neither do they!"

NOT BILL'S SUIT

Mom, who had dementia and three husbands, the last of whom was Bill who died in 2016, came out with an old man's suit from her closet. She asked me if I thought my husband would want it. (Ha! It's from the seventies and way too small.) I said, "I don't think so, but thanks, Mom, and where did you get that suit?"

She said, "It was Bill's."

I said, "I don't think so, Mom."

She replied, "I know it is; I buried him in it!"

"Umm—how'd you get that suit back?" Even she had to laugh.

BEANS

My dad was in the hospital and he was a fall risk. So when Dad was placed in the hospital recliner, the nurses had first placed an alarm that would sound if Dad tried to get up.

Well, Dad would raise up on the recliner enough to get the alarm to sound, then announce, "Darn beans."

EGGS AND AN ONION

I had just gotten off the phone with my eighty-year-old biological father. His eighty-one-year-old wife was supposed to be released from the hospital that day after a procedure to repair several fractured back vertebrae. (Ouch.) It is a long story, but this was her third time being hospitalized for it but her first time for the procedure.

My dad said, "I told her she needs to nail down when she's going to be released and let us know right now. You've got a schedule; I've got a schedule. Neither of us can just jump in the car and go get her!" (The hospital is less than two miles from his home and about eight miles from mine. Yes, we can.)

I tried not to laugh. He's been retired (probably not a wise choice) since he was fifty-one. He can drive his nasty, rusty old pickup truck when he's not dizzy, and she prefers riding in that to being in my lower sports car. Best I can tell, he sits around watching TV or buying miracle cures off the internet all day, every day.

I asked, "Why not, Dad?"

He said the damn doctors need to get their act together and let the family know exactly when the patient will be released. "People have things to do!"

In a gentle way, I asked him what he needed to do. "Well, maybe I don't have so many things to do but I do need to get over to that damn grocery store and pick up some eggs and an onion—if I don't feel dizzy." I've bought and delivered almost all their groceries since I moved them there the previous October. No, he doesn't need to do that.

I can see his obvious anxiety about picking her up and him needing to up his game on partner care but I just found his approach to it so funny!

MAKE THE INEVITABLE SPECIAL

I will tell you as I reflect on caregiving—I'm a product of the adage, "It takes a village to raise a child," but it also takes a village to care for itself. I think my earliest days of dealing with death started with my great-grandmother, who was an Eastern Star (easternstar.org). I remember her passing and how big of a deal it was. Certainly, It was very painful to my grandmother and very painful to my mother, but I was a child sort of bearing witness to this process that would later be called death and understood that it was one of the finalities of life. But what was very interesting was how we celebrated death and her being an Eastern Star. All these women lined up in formation, going into the home-going rituals, one at a time. So that made me fascinated with this thing called death and it didn't seem at all painful. It seemed very formal, and it seemed part of the process of life. I had seen the end part but by the time my grandmother passed, I saw some of the other parts of the process that led up to death.

It started with a stroke. And that first stroke sort of took her voice away, and that was it. Her movement on the right side of her body was gone. Her movement was now very limited and much of a struggle. And I watched my family gather around her. Certainly, my mother was a nurse and comfortable with caring for people, but that was her work. She had to go and do her job, so the rest of the family had to do it.

What I used to do for my grandmother, at the time, was to go and soak her feet, and I would scrape her feet and cut her toenails. I would also comb her hair because she was always this very fashionable woman, and her hair was everything. As she was moving on in age, her hair got very brittle, and I started to see more of this gray hair, predominantly gray hair, but how wiry it was, and I would sit with her, which was my role. I sat next to her, and I loved her. She made sounds that you had to understand as responses to questions. When she wanted something, it was a certain sound, and she could say some limited words, and that was it.

Being by her bedside was the first time I realized the kind of care you have to be prepared to give someone. And that is to pick up where they can no longer do those things for themselves. If they can do it for themselves, you want them to do it for themselves, but someone has to be there if they can't. And so that was my role until the time she left.

After that, there was a lot of death in the family. I didn't have much to do with it. I started to lose my uncles. I have to give my Mom a lot of credit because she was really the anchor in death. She was the one who ensured that everything was attended to.

And so now, here we are, fast forward. I am now watching my mother age out. I travel a lot, so when I get home, I'm clear that something has changed. Probably more than my sisters and brothers because they are right with her, and it's so gradual that you don't know it. But when I walked into the room, I saw everything that had gradually changed that I didn't bear witness to.

So, I started to notice my mother making these shaking gestures. They were mild, but clearly, she was losing control of her hand. And then I began to think, wait a minute. You know Mom is getting old. What kind of conversations should she and I have? I've been that son that makes her comfortable, the one that she can trust to protect her, that I do hear her. I will agree with her sometimes, and any disagreements with her are not designed to make her feel like a child but to help her understand there's a better approach than maybe what she's thinking about.

I also had to help her feel less afraid and feel okay with what she was going through. It's scary. My mother is a devout Christian, and one day, she asked me a question, "What do you believe is going to happen when you die?". I said you've been a devout Christian, and you've been studying this and believing in this life after death. It may be what you've believed, but do you question it now? She said, "You get to this point, and you're not sure." So, there's still this scariness there, and I think it's important to help her come to terms with the life process when she finds herself there.

She's watched everybody else go, and now she understands that she's on her way out. She's not fatally ill, thank goodness. Still, she's had several illnesses, including a light heart attack, her kidneys beginning to fail, and sometimes there's a question about her memory and now the Parkinsons. That's a lot for a woman in her eighties who is so used to being in control and now realizing that she no longer can be completely in control.

I think part of caregiving is determining how

you make a comfortable space, one that they can say, I know I'm unable to do these things. Still, I know someone's got me on this, and I know it's not just someone doing it for me, but it's somebody who loves me, someone who will give their life for me, making it less scary. It's like holding someone's hand you trust when going off a cliff's edge.

I make that more important than anything I say to or do for her. I need her to have the right mind space, and I think that's about mental health issues because it starts to play with older people psychologically. The loneliness and just knowing that this is a journey of no return.

Part of it is the discussion, but then there are those other things because I see people not preparing for what happens when it's all said and done. I decided to have these wonderful conversations with my mother about death, but we also talked about life. Things like, what her fondest memories were and the things she feels she has accomplished in her life that she would like to have left as a legacy. I joke with her about "Who really was your favorite kid; you can say it off the record. I'll be sure not to tell them." We get to a conversation that will allow her to be reflective, to think about the things she can do, and to share those things that she thinks are important.

But how do we ensure that everything has been important because her life has been about her kids, her legacy, and certainly, her friends and family? We talk not only about funds; I have a list of what she feels is important. She talks to me about money. She brought up some bonds I didn't know she had. She went through the entire house and asked who should have what. I have a list of what she sees as assets, where her bank accounts and other assets are. She talked about their history, where she got them from, and who she would want to receive them.

She talked about her jewelry. We have videoed everything, including silverware and china, and her speaking to the person she'd like to give it to. So, when I give my niece the jewelry my mother would like, I will provide her with the video from my mother talking about the pieces she is leaving. "I wanted you to have these things; this is where I got them from, the history. This is why they are special, and this is why I want to give them to you."

When I go to Miami, I go for her. I hang out with her for the last precious moments I can have with her. I don't know when the last visit will be. It may be ten years down the road, but part of that is helping her to move through this part of her life.

We are figuring it out. What about her insurance papers, the deed on the house, and any outstanding arrangements? That takes that out of her head and out of her mind. She's not trying to figure out what to do with it. We're doing it together, so it's no longer necessary for her to worry about it. She knows that when the end comes, there's clarity. She knows what her church will get and what her family members will get.

Dealing with her sickness was difficult. It was hard for her to come to terms with the fact that she has Parkinson's. She had been trying to hide that from me. Her right side has major tremors. But I didn't know because she would hold her right hand, stabilizing it. During one of my visits, something happened, the phone was ringing, it was my sister, and she wasn't answering. Why wasn't she answering?

She had to let go of that hand when she reached for the phone, and I saw the tremors.

I asked her what was happening, and she decided to tell me what was not happening with her. She said,

"I went to the Doctor, and it's not Parkinson's." I said, "Mom, it's not Parkinson's, but clearly, it's something. Did the doctor tell you what it is, and you're minimizing it?" She replied, "No." I said, "When you go to the doctor again, you tell her that your son said, if she does not refer you to a neurologist, I will take you to one for evaluation. We're going to figure this out. Once we know what it is, we can manage it.' Once she received the first statement that it wasn't what she feared, she needed no more talk about it.

So, the doctor sent her to another doctor, and they confirmed it was Parkinson's. Once she heard that, she became depressed. We started talking about clinical trials. I reached out to the Parkinson's Association. We talked about medication. A clinical trial happened to be going on at the University of Miami. I registered her in the trial because they were trying to figure out how to make the medication better. They already had a medication, and they were trying to improve the side effects. They felt that combining that medication with another would result in continuing the helpful impact that would manage the Parkinsons.

Because my Mom read that one of the side effects could be that she would be prone to falling, she declined the trial, saying, "I don't know if, at this age, I want to be falling, which can lead to hip issues." We put her on another Parkinson's medication that is helping her. My Mom and I also talk about the "little things" that would make her comfortable as she nears the end and may be unable to communicate, like keeping her feet warm and ensuring she is "made up" nicely.

I go home every three weeks, and I stay with her. We are trying to see how to manage some things legally. I am moving fast because we don't know when other medical issues might emerge. It's about getting things done. My siblings and I have arranged everything so all documents are in place and the correct people are nearby. Should anything happen, there will not be the need to wait for me to fly in. Concerning me, I've taken care of all documents and have everything in a place my siblings know about. They will not have to worry about or figure out anything. Going through this with a parent is enlightening. I've also been blessed to have mentors who I've seen and helped go through this. As a Black man, I am fortunate to have had many older Black men who have helped me in life and shared this time with me.

When we understand that death is a part of life, we start to plan for it. Many of us will not accept this and will "psyche" ourselves out that we will live forever. If we do all we can do in this life, approaching the end of life is not so scary. We have a right to make this a special time, to make it joyful.

IT BECAME APPARENT

My caregiving journey began six years ago. My Mom went to the doctor regularly, but then she started going more frequently. What was brought to my attention by the receptionist when we went to the doctor's office, was that my mother's medical insurance was no longer active. My mother was retired and had always kept her insurance premiums paid.

When I called the insurance company, I discovered her payments were three months behind. I knew then that something was wrong physically and mentally. I had to reactivate her insurance. Thankfully, in the seventeen years of her retirement, she had never been late with a payment. Her premiums were paid faithfully and on time. I then decided that she should not go to the doctor unaccompanied because, like all parents, she tended to hide her illnesses from her children.

I began to go to the doctor with her so that I would know the nature of her decline concerning her physical and cognitive functioning and who I had to look for with regard to her care. I was informed that she was diagnosed with myelodysplasia syndrome (MDS). Her red blood cell count was severely low. The doctor indicated that, had my mother's white blood cells not been fine, she would have advanced into full-blown leukemia.

My mother has a family history of cancer. All of her brothers died of cancer, her older sister is cancer-free, and my mother had no cancer. She was subjected to weekly shots, which, to me, is a form of chemotherapy. The doctor informed me that I would have to give the shots at home. I was terrified—I don't like needles.

I declined that approach but took Mom to the doctor every week. My poor Mom felt like a pin cushion. Her veins were difficult to access. I was becoming anxious and upset. They were moving from veins in the arm to veins in the hand, which was very painful. I gave up my full-time position and took one that was part-time to take care of her. I retained my pastorate at the church because I could do it from home. I had control of the schedule, and I had a co-pastor.

The first major incident was Mom's heart attack, which occurred around 2016 following the death of her brother. We did not know that he was in stage 4 lung cancer until he passed away. Neither Mom's sister-in-law nor her brother's children shared information. Mom's heart attack resulted in her having to share information about her other medical difficulties she had not told me about. Now, I had to meet her cardiologist and her nephrologist.

So now we had a triumvirate with whom I had to confer and schedule appointments. Because of the heart attack and the MDS, I had to monitor her oxygen levels. Her doctor told me that I had to take Mom to the hospital for a transfusion if the levels dropped below a certain level. I also knew I had to take care of myself to ensure I'd be there to care for her.

Thankfully, I had no major health issues, just a little bit of blood pressure problems. I told the doctor that, though the blood pressure was a genetic issue, I never had high numbers because I monitored what I ate. However, while caring for my Mom, I was not as diligent about my food choices, and I exercised. The doctor prescribed medication for me, but I did not take it regularly because my numbers were not high.

I was scared to death about taking Mom to the hospital because it was during the COVID-19 pandemic. I took her to the same hospital all the time so that we would not have to go through the testing to determine her health condition. Her cardiologists were there. She ultimately had to have a pacemaker inserted. My Mom was a strong lady.

I never had a problem at the hospital because a friend of mine was there. He promised to intercede if I ever had any problems. It was comforting to know that he was there and that the hospital was close to the house. The EMT workers told me that ten minutes made a difference in addressing cardiac emergencies.

The nephrologist told me of her kidney problems, and she was prescribed a lot of medication as a result. I was concerned about that because I felt that any kind of weakness in her body would be made worse by synthetic medications. I made sure that everything she ate was organic.

She developed psoriasis. I took her to the dermatologist, but everything he tried did not work, and because it was during COVID-19, it would take two months to get an appointment. I said, "Enough of this!", and took her to my dermatologist, who explained everything to me in detail and assured me that it was not contagious.

Over time, she became feistier. I was the only caregiver around her. My brother, who lived upstate, tried taking her to his home to give me a break. After a while, my Mom did not want to go, feeling that she was left alone while he worked. That hurt him. She could go out when she was with me to dinner, plays, or other activities. But she really preferred to be at home with me.

She did not want a home attendant because she did not want anyone in her "things." We had visiting nurse services come to check on her occasionally. But the interesting thing is that whenever she had to go to the hospital on an emergency basis, I had EMTs and firemen traipsing through my house.

The only respite I had was that sometimes when she was in the hospital, her church members would go and sit with her and would tell me not to feel that it was an imposition to request their help. My mother was a Deacon and continued with that until she could no longer participate. I supported her through the decline in her physical functioning.

When I went out, my cousin came, and then ultimately, my baby brother moved in and could watch her. He would eat with her in the evening, and she and my brother conspired to increase her consumption of sugared items (candy, soda, etc.). Though she was supposed to have one small can of soda a day, he would purchase more for her. When I confronted him about it, he asked, "How did you know I bought it?" and I replied, "Because Mom ratted you out!" He asked Mom why she told on him, and she replied, "Because you would buy it, and you're a sucker!"

Clearly, Mom's capacity to restrain her responses had declined. Though she was still very "lady-like," sometimes she just said what was on her mind. Once I resolved one issue, another one emerged. I wound up having to provide personal care. I took her to her hair appointments, and my brother would give her pedicures. She was forbidden to lift anything over three pounds. She would get up in the middle of the night and partake of my brother's snacks. He caught her one night, and he started to buy more.

Mom waited for me to leave the country before

"going home" (passing away) in July of 2022. I visited her in the hospital the night before. I fed her dinner and went home to pack. I had to take a 6 a.m. flight to Mexico to perform a wedding, so I had to be at the airport at 4 a.m. On the plane, getting ready to take off, though it was in airplane mode, my phone rang. It was my brother calling to say my mother had transitioned. When I landed in Mexico, I knew my mother, and I knew she would say, "I'm not going anywhere, do what you have to do. I performed the wedding. I did not cry until I got to my room that night.

CAREGIVING "P" AND "C": PRIVILEGE AND CHALLENGE

The caregiving journey with my mother, Jean, who is now eighty-four years old and will be eighty-five in November, started when she was about seventy-six or seventy-seven, somewhere around there. I think she'd had some surgeries before her seventy-fifth birthday. That's kind of the marker for us because my sisters and I made a gift of a trip to China for her and her partner when she turned seventy-five. One of our cousins, who is part of the diplomatic corps for

Trinidad, was actually working at the office in China, and my mother said she was interested in going.

So, we kind of heard her talking and decided to surprise her. She had had, at this point, one spinal surgery, and I think it was a successful rehab, and she was doing some other work. She started walking with a walker, then with a cane and then was unassisted. She went over to China, and on the second day, she was unable to walk, which was just incredible. So, she left walking and came back in a wheelchair. They connected her with some Chinese doctors and acupuncturists and tried to do some work to help with any pain or discomfort she was having, to no avail. She had to change her flight, even to fly her back so she could lie down.

It was from there that other things started, and she had another surgery, which kind of alleviated some problems but then led to other problems. The "undoing" was probably related to some strokes. There might have been more based on some things she told me that happened, but we counted about twelve mini-strokes.

Her speech was a little slurry. But sometimes, she sounds like that in the mornings anyway. But you know, I was talking to her in the morning and noticed that the sound changed. It's almost as if someone was like a soprano, and they became a tenor, so the timber changed. I asked, why does your voice sound like that? She said, "I don't know, it just started happening; I don't know what happened."

I called her doctor, and we talked, and I said, "Oh, you listen to her voice." So, he listencd. Then he asked her some questions, and she could answer them. I told him that this was unusual, that this sudden change had happened. He said, well, you're right to be concerned. He said I think she should come in, so I took her in the car. We drove into Manhattan. After about, I guess, nine hours or so, they finally found a tiny bleed and, of course, confirmed that it was, in fact, a stroke. Of course, with the tiny ones, not much can be done. You monitor it, and you may see some things. They kept her in the hospital.

We've been the tag team; we're taking turns. In terms of her care, I think we've always been close, my sisters and I, but this has brought us closer in many ways and has helped us address our own health and our own lives and try to navigate a little differently. It's been a journey, and I'm somewhat sad. I remember the first day I noticed something was happening and was extremely upset. Because it almost feels like you're kind of helpless, you don't know what to do, and it isn't easy.

But the plus I see in all of this is that I've spent more time with my mother than ever as an adult. The pandemic, of course, helped that as well. We spent a lot of time together and talked a lot, and we rode around together so she could get out.

I've done some work on my house and my yard just so that she is able to get out and enjoy some air. We watch movies outside and have a good time. I find that if she's in good spirits, it ends up being a very good day for her. She has some close friends, one in particular who is like one of the aunties I've known all my life. I'll pick her up sometimes and bring her out, then they'll visit, and then we'll all do something together. That seems to brighten her day.

As far as I can tell from this journey, besides taking care of her, I think our role as her children is to ensure her spirits stay up. Also, we should show up as enthusiastically as possible rather than seem like this is a downer. What's been helpful is that my sister, in New Jersey, is here every week.

Some people helped take care of Mom during the day. We ultimately retained an agency, but that was the first thing before that. Someone from one of my churches asked if I needed help, and I said yes. I said, "Well, you should come by and meet Mom." They met and hit it off. So, she was here for a while, and we were using someone from the agency in the evenings.

People from the agency kept not working out, however. If someone new were assigned, I'd have to be around to make sure that they were appropriately acclimated so that there would be no errors, especially around transferring her from the wheelchair; from the bed to the wheelchair, the wheelchair to the toilet, and back out of the bathroom.

So, that became a greater challenge. Then, the caregiver from the church said that her daughter did this work professionally, so she was licensed, etc. And that the daughter said she needed an evening job. By the way, I'd known both of them for over thirty years, and they were fantastic.

I say this is God's hand because, you know, you think about sharing your needs with the universe and then getting these answers back. So, this was the godsend. As a matter of fact, one of them, the daughter, is here now; the mother retired recently,

Mom's lived there for a number of years and owned apartments in that building for a few years. There are so many of the people who've lived there, of course, who have now reached the age of becoming senior citizens, and so in their aging, a naturally occurring retirement community has formed. There's a really robust program with meetings and activities, and they're supported through the New York City Department of Aging and a few other agencies.

Through that connection, there's a caregiver support group for adult children who care for their parents. It's been fantastic in terms of those conversations. And, of course, I'm in one-on-one therapy, as well.

Well, I believe that the mind is the first place that we can direct the rest of everything else. So, I think it's helpful to have those discussions and just be able to share. It's beneficial to have another who listens, especially as the person who needs help is the ear for many other people. In a way, where there's no worry about what's going to happen to me like there would be if I shared certain things with family members, therapy becomes important, which is helpful.

So, this is the journey. As I said to someone, I still call this a privilege because I get to hold her hand during these times of what could be the final stages of life on this side. And so, I understand, and I get that we're in a special place in that I get to talk about all kinds of things before it's too late. I believe this is a privilege in a lot of ways.

My mother sometimes asks me things like, "What would I do if I didn't have you?" And then she says to me, "I think you guys are doing too much, spending too much money. Why don't you just put me somewhere and just, you know, let this go?" and I reply, "That's not gonna' happen," because of course, I think no matter what she says, that's not really what she wants.

We remind her that she's the one who ensured we were here. We were all immigrants from Trinidad. She came to New York to work as a nurse because she was recruited from a hospital in Trinidad. When she was settled, she brought my dad, then my two sisters and me, and next our grandparents, and then an aunt to her youngest sister. Our youngest sister was born here in the mid-seventies. Mom ensured that many things were handled, including education, when it was time to move, and purchasing a house.

It was her drive that made so much happen. My father's a lot lower-key about a lot of things. I tell her this, and she starts crying when I recall the stories because she'll remember. I'd tell her, "Your harvest is here because you've done all this sowing. This is your harvest, Sister. Enjoy this time, and we'll have a good time and give you the best care possible."

Mom had a suitor who stopped coming around. I tend not to react immediately—I just listened to his position. He talked about being unable to handle seeing her, unlike the person he was used to seeing. I get what that is. Some of my friends had names to attach to that behavior and other things about him, but I said, "I'm clear this is not what he signed up for. I'm also clear that you have to meet people where they are, and you can't expect somebody to be someone different if this is who they are."

And I think from the whole family's perspective, they were together and very active for more than twenty years. We were all clear about who he was, but that was also her choice. Respecting his situation was not my battle, so we went on and did what had to be done. At this point, the focus is ensuring we honor our mother and do the right things for her.

I find the one thing we need as caregivers is trust-worthy people. It's so much the dilemma where there is a constant search; someone still needs to stay overnight. As a music maker who still creates and performs, I have had to curtail my performing life in many ways because even with the agency, my general rule is that I don't accept jobs on the nights when I know I will be too far away. I've installed a lot of technology around Mom, so I can look in, communicate, and summon help if needed.

When I'm out of the house (I tend not to go any-more), I am fifteen or twenty minutes away in case I have to get back here quickly and tend to her at night after the last person leaves. So, the immediate and ongoing need is someone who's trustworthy and can be here at night.

My sister did a lot of research before we retained the current agency. The number one choice didn't have available personnel when we started looking. The number two choice is actually the one we settled with, and they send people, but sometimes the people are ill-equipped to do the work. If someone new comes in, I sit in my office on the second floor. So most days, I work from home to keep an eye on what's going on.

But then, if someone new is starting, I have to be much more engaged and less focused on my work because I want to ensure they are handling things appropriately. I have to make sure they don't drop her or make bad decisions.

I've heard some horror stories. I have a good friend who wasn't the primary caregiver, but his sister was. Their mother died from cancer complications, and I remembered that, in two instances, she had suffered falls at the hands of less attentive people. That's disturbing, and of course, that's my ongoing nightmare.

So, finding a trustworthy person who can actually work overnight would be an amazing help. Also, I think my sleep has been impeded because I do not have an overnight person. I'm a light sleeper anyway, and I wouldn't say I like sleeping much anyway. Even so, sleep is necessary.

Sometimes, during the night, my Mom wakes up confused, and I hear her laughing. The person who was caring for her might have left some crazy show on TV or something. If I don't realize it, she mixes that story with a dream and then thinks something else is happening. I'll have to sit with her for a while, but by the time she goes back to sleep, it takes me a couple of hours before I settle down to sleep again. This is how it goes.

I don't have as much of a problem on the weekends because I have started her nightly routine. When this all started, she attended church every weekend, every Sunday. I began by arranging for someone to take her to church after the first stroke happened. It automatically took away the consideration of her driving. Her decline was a slow progression, but it does take a village.

The other piece that is difficult for caregivers that I've noticed, and which I've discussed at length in therapy and in groups, is where there have been issues between the caregiver and their parent. It is difficult to find peace with that and actually to do this work.

People are often surprised because, of course, I'm serving as music director for three churches and one Catholic university, so a lot is going on. Listening to some of the people in the group, there are those who had issues with their parents, especially in the years before they became incapacitated. There is a very common thread regarding how one reconciles that part of the story, so they are enabled or empowered to do and give their best caregiving.

Thank God I've started having longer conversations with my sisters, particularly the one I see weekly. We have talked more, and I made it a point that we have the same primary care doctors so that we can discuss conditions and look at what things we might have in common and what we might actually be able to do differently. I think it requires a lot of intention where this is concerned.

And then, of course, we discussed that I have no children, so who will care for me? I bought long-term care insurance, and there's a good deal of life insurance, but I'm just making sure my sisters know I have these in place when the time comes.

3

LIFETIME GOALS

"One of the lessons that I grew up with was to always stay true to yourself and never let what somebody else says distract you from your goals. And so when I hear about negative and false attacks, I really don't invest any energy in them, because I know who I am." –Michelle Obama[1]

IT WAS IMPORTANT

MY DAD WAS in and out of the hospital from 2011 to 2013. He had a myriad of issues. In 2011, he was in the hospital when I called him. He was slurring his words and was difficult to understand. He had received an endoscopy, during which there was a puncture and following which my dad had a ministroke. This was the beginning of a series of medical events.

At some point, my father came to live with me (though he did not want to). I cleared a bedroom, a sitting room, and a bathroom on the other side of the living room in my apartment. Dad stayed with me for four months, during which I hired a home caregiver to care for him while I continued to work.

Dad eventually went home but was rehospitalized from August to October 2013 following an additional stroke, after which he was unable to speak.

On one of my visits with Dad, he was trying to tell me something. I could not understand him. I continued to talk and let him know I had brought his mail with me. At this point, he became more animated and as I went through the mail with him, his gesturing increased. He was distraught and began pounding on the envelopes. Finally, we got to the envelope for home insurance and he pounded. I told him I had already paid the bill. He immediately calmed down and was obviously relieved. He was fearful that his assets were not protected. Even at this point, he was focused on making certain that things were financially taken care of.

FOUR YEARS AND A VILLAGE

We finished our dissertations within one year of each other, supporting each other through the process. We both set out specific professional goals. Along the way, marriages came and went. She was blessed with a child for whom she made every sacrifice to ensure she would be successful.

She went for a physical exam and was told to have further evaluation. She was ultimately diagnosed with stage four breast cancer. At the same time, she was offered the job of her dreams in another state. "Should I take it?" she wondered out loud.

"Of course," I exclaimed without hesitation. This was after realizing the support needed to accomplish her success in the new position.

She took her new position and began chemotherapy shortly thereafter. Her new staff was fiercely supportive of her as she worked through the cancer treatments. They assured her transportation and made certain the appropriate technology was in place to enable her to do her job. She made a huge impact and was celebrated for her innovations. Her friends decided to provide support for her, and though they were in another state, they flew in regularly to spend time with her throughout the almost two-year period of chemotherapy and radiation.

She was cleared of cancer until its return four years after its initial diagnosis. Her friends gathered to assist with packing and the move back to her home state. She passed away shortly thereafter.

THE KINDNESS OF LOVED ONES

I traveled to the Caribbean and upon my evening return (about 8:00 p.m.), without my request, my parents decided to pick me up. My father had dementia but was still driving. When we went out to the car, it was gone. My father had parked in an illegal area outside the terminal and so the saga began.

We hailed a cab and were taken to the office of the folks who towed at JFK airport. They had not towed the car but the Port Authority at JFK had. One of the truck drivers at the initial tow office was kind enough to take us to the Port Authority building. I had my parents take a seat while I went to the office, where the man in charge explained he could not accept cash, check, or credit card. One had to pay with a money order. (I can only assume that most people give up at this point, leave their car, and pay the additional fee for having it kept at the facility overnight.)

He quoted the amount of the payment. I left my parents, now huddled in their seats on a bench, caught cab number two, and traveled about three miles to a check-cashing location at a gas station on Van Wyck Expressway in Queens. I got the money order and returned to the office, only to learn the money order was incorrectly made for an amount in excess of what was needed. I stated that I really did not mind the overpayment and would sign to that effect. I was advised that this was not possible; the money order had to be precisely the amount of the fee.

I left the office and hailed cab number three, returned to the check-cashing facility, and then returned to the Port Authority office, where my parents continued to wait in the outer seating area. I paid the fee and my father's car was identified in the outside lot. The ordeal had taken four hours! I drove them home, thanked them for trying, and suggested it would be best that I take a cab in the future.

I was fortunate my parents were still ambulatory and they were kind enough to drive to the airport to pick me up. However, following this event, something like this effort could no longer be attempted by them.

4

PARANOIA

*"The trick to aging gracefully is
to enjoy it." –Unknown*

THEY CAME WITH LARGE BLACK BAGS

A FRIEND WAS CARING for her mother at the same time I began the process of caring for my mom. Her mother and mine talked on the phone extensively about the hired female caregivers, cleaners, etc., who came to people's homes, always with large black bags. Their conclusion was that they brought them so they could steal items from people's homes.

My friend and I laughed regularly about this mindset. One day, she called and said, "Well, here is the latest: My mother is accusing the lady of stealing the plastic uncovered butter dish that came with the refrigerator. I had to let her know that I replaced it with a glass covered butter dish."

Laughing, I replied, "You may have outdone me. The latest here is that one glass (old, worn, and later found to be broken and discarded) was stolen from the cupboard."

Finding humor in what can become trying little circumstances is required for caregiving, as this wariness is likely to continue for some period of time in the some who are elderly. When humor no longer softens a particular situation, patience and attention to detail are needed as in the following story.

THE MISSING LAUNDRY

Last fall, my mom told us her aide returned from the laundromat with both sheets and one pillow-case. We are not sure how many pillowcases were sent to wash.

About six months later, my mom told a new aide that two pillowcases and a comforter were lost at the laundromat. This new aide was asked to go to the laundromat but was told not to take a certain bath towel. When the aide returned, that towel was not where it had last been seen. The aide was asked by my mom why she took the towel when she had asked her not to, because now the towel was missing. We can only surmise that when the aide left to go to the laundromat, Mom hid it (as she had been doing with other items).

Mom decided to wash her sheets and hang them outside in the middle of winter. She hung the sheets outside during the day and went to bring them in that night, in 20°F weather. The door slammed shut behind her and there was no exit from the rear yard. Thankfully, her grandson lived in the downstairs apartment and again thankfully, he was home and heard the banging on his back door. He said she had on her pajamas and the sheets, which were as stiff as cardboard, were around her shoulders.

When she was called and confronted about being stubborn, she said God was not ready for her and hung up the phone.

Fortunately, this mother's difficult behavior was with laundry, specifically the bedding. Some other habits and behaviors make caregiving much more expensive and all-consuming.

I served as caregiver for my sister, Barbara, for about four years before she passed. Barbara was seventy-eight years old and suffered from Alzheimer's disease. She was also a diabetic who never met a piece of cheesecake she did not love.

Barbara was admitted to the hospital for a surgical procedure. Her doctor's orders included "nothing by mouth" that evening. During the night she had a bad dream and hallucinated that the nurses were outside her room planning to poison her. Although she was not supposed to be given a meal that night, for some unexplained reason a tray with a meal and dessert was left at her bedside.

When the food service supervisor learned the patient was given a food tray the night before, she was upset with the night shift staff. My sister told her she had not touched the food because she heard the nurses planning to poison her. Nonetheless, in the interest of safety her surgery was rescheduled.

I stayed on to calm her and reassure her that her nurse was not trying to kill her and did not poison her food. When she calmed down, I prepared to leave and say a prayer with her as we always did. As I held her hands, which were under her covers,

I felt something strange. When I lifted the covers, I could see she was holding on to a wrapped serving of cheesecake I asked her why, for a woman so upset because she believed someone had poisoned her food, did she keep the cheesecake from the tray. She looked at me and loudly replied, "Evidence."

SEEK AND YE SHALL FIND

Recently, Mom has been looking for, and finding, black things in her food, on the floor, in the sink, on the table—just about everywhere. Needless to say, she is the only one who can see them and tells us *our* eyes are bad. She insists on examining oatmeal, flour, grains, eggs, and paper products and removing anything suspect. What's more, she and everything in her orbit are *electrified, indoctrinated, infiltrated,* and *inundated.*

She doesn't trust anything that's purchased locally, or food that's stored in the downstairs freezer. Food that's good one day is bad the next. Coffee is a routine problem; she can't get the right taste and is always asking one of us to buy a good can of coffee. Water has to be boiled—orange and other juices too. Preparing nutritious meals that appeal to her and that she will eat is a major challenge and source of frustration.

Her "craziness" is unpredictable, and she seems to reserve it for the caregivers, especially when we're at home. We never know what we're gonna get or when we're gonna get it. When company comes or when we're out of the house—in public, at church, or with extended family—Mom is her most charming and lovable self. Even at home, there *are* wonderful moments, days, or parts of the day when we have our mom back—the sweet, caring, compassionate, loving, vibrant, highly accomplished, astute, and intelligent woman who raised us with unconditional love. These times are all the more precious, all the more cherished.

5

DEALING WITH MEDICAL AND LEGAL ISSUES

"Whatever is bringing you down, get rid of it. Because you'll find that when you're free, your true creativity, your true self comes out." –**Tina Turner**[2]

THE SPEAKING ENGAGEMENT: AN EXERCISE IN FOCUS AND CALM

ONE FOOT WAS out of the car as I caught a glimpse of my colleague crossing the street on the way to a panel discussion in which we were both participating. My cell phone rang. It was the internist who was seeing my mother for a flu shot.

"Hi, this is Dr. One (not his name). Have you noticed some deterioration in your mother's functioning?" he asked.

As I drew my foot back into the car, I hesitantly commented that I noticed some increase in difficulty with speech (she does have aphasia after all). He went on to say that he noted a significant change. "She's different," he stated. I hung up with Dr. One and called my sister, who had been scheduling my mother's medical appointments.

We agreed we'd have to move up the appointment with Dr. Two, the neurologist. (It had been scheduled for many weeks later.) My sister hung up to call Dr. Two.

I called back Dr. One, asking, "Is she in the room with you?"

"Yes," he replied. I began to anticipate how upset Mom might be with his having identified her deteriorated functioning.

Just then, my sister called back to say, "I reached Dr. Two's office, and they will call on Monday to let us know if Mom can come in that day." (Needless to say Monday was Columbus Day, a work holiday. Another one "bites the dust."

I got out of the car and proceeded to the panel. Seated comfortably, I adjusted my cell phone to vibrate. The panel discussion began. Five minutes in, my phone vibrated with a text message. College A (the college one of my nieces attends) is on lockdown due to a possible live shooter, but she is safe and okay. The panel discussion continued and luckily, I was on autopilot but fully focused and engaged.

At the end of the lively and well-received discussion, I dropped my colleague back at the office. Next, because I was unable to even think about starting on any work project at the office, I directed my car home so I could see what emotional condition my mother was in following her doctor's visit. She was happy and "chirping," letting me know it was just "little things" Dr. One was referring to.

By the way, the young man on the campus who was thought to have a gun actually had an umbrella.

ONE DOCTOR'S APPLE IS
ANOTHER DOCTOR'S ORANGE

Continuing from the previous story, Dr. One's intern had administered a mini-mental-status exam and the results indicated moderately severe cognitive impairment. The test also indicated that my mother was disoriented. When I looked at the test results, as a psychologist, I knew the test had not been administered appropriately, nor had my mother's aphasia (resulting from a stroke in 2009) been taken into account. Though I knew this, I pressed forward with the appointment with Dr. Two because under no circumstances would I act as my mother's doctor or decline to follow up with her neurologist given Dr. One's alarm.

On Columbus Day morning, as I was completing office work on the computer, my sister called to inform me that Dr. Two's office was checking to see if there was a cancellation so Mom could come in. I shared with my sister the need for a two-hour window to enable preparation to leave the house and get to the appointment. (This is an area of growth for me. I would not have made my needs known in the past.) At 10:00 a.m., my sister called back to say, "You have your two-hour window." I asked that she call my mother to let her know. (My mother's reaction to *anything* new or sudden is characterized by agitation and fussing.)

I dropped my work and prepared to leave the house. At 11:00 a.m., my mother came to my door to see if I was ready. (This is the "disoriented" lady who cannot be rushed.) I told her I'd be down shortly. As I descended the stairs, my mother asked as usual whether I had something warm to put on. I replied that I had a scarf (worn as a shawl) and off we went.

When I got out of the car near the doctor's office, the scarf had disappeared. Oh well, I probably dropped it in the driveway. (Another instance of being distracted while attending to Mom's needs.) Arriving at the building where the doctor was located, I suggested Mom lead the way, which she did, with full confidence and no difficulties. She located the correct elevator and knew the right floor.

We sat in the waiting area and Mom went for reading material for both of us. Within a few minutes, she was called in to the doctor's office and I rose to accompany her.

"I don't know why you are going in," she stated. "Oh, but I am," I said and smiled as we walked into the office. (There was no way I could allow this visit to happen without having full clarity on Dr. Two's impressions.)

Dr. Two was a joy to watch as he interacted with Mom, weaving in the mental status examination while talking about current events, the status of politics in New York, stories about one of his daughters, work experiences, etc. By the end of the visit, he concluded that Dr. One's findings were inaccurate and did not take into account Mom's aphasia. I made sure he had updated telephone information for my sister and me. He indicated we could call him anytime.

We drove home, chatting along the way. When we got home, there was the scarf. Someone had placed it on the knob of Mom's door.

AND I AM SUPPOSED TO DO WHAT?

A guy I know was very close to his father, who had a heart attack. He took his dad to the ER, where he died shortly after arrival. As this guy was trying to personally process what just happened, he was told he had to get his dad out of there right away. When he told me the story, he talked about how sadly crazy it was. He said he thought, *what am I going to do? Drive him around in the car?*

CAREGIVER RANT TURNED FUNNY STORY

So today, we had a follow-up appointment with my grandmother's surgeon following her hip replacement surgery back in July. When we went to the appointment in August, the surgeon placed her in another four weeks of physical therapy because she hadn't met her goal of walking without a walker.

The problem is that her neurologist is the one who recommended she keep a walker twenty-four/seven due to poor balance issues with Parkinson's disease. She's an extreme fall risk and has even said herself that she's more secure on her own feet than with the walker. The physical therapist basically had to spell out for the surgeon that she needed to keep the walker.

But here's the thing: Grandmother got completely hung up on them saying she should be able to walk without a walker. It took me *weeks* to convince her that yes, the one doctor the one time told her she should be able to walk without a walker but the other three doctors/specialists (general practitioner, physical therapist, and neurologist) who knew her better suggested she keep the walker, so that's what we're doing.

Fast forward to this morning, prior to the appointment. When filling out my grandmother's paperwork, I asked the nurse to quietly remind the doctor *not* to mention that she "could" be without a walker. Sure, she could. But she could break her other hip or more during her next fall. She gave me a knowing smile, slipped around the corner, and gave a quick whisper to the doctor.

So imagine my angst when the X-ray tech said, "Hey, look at you! You don't need that silly walker; it's just slowing you down. Toss that thing!"

I could feel the "oh shit; this will take weeks to undo" feeling creep up until Grandmother delivered the perfect line: "Don't you let my granddaughter hear you say that. It'll give her a coronary."

So caregivers, nurses, doctors, etc.: if you don't know the full scope of your patient's needs, please don't comment on how they could do without the cane or walker.

However, this was the best laugh I'd had in a while. Laughter is the best medicine and finding humor in a situation does help ease the stress of caregiving.

WHAT THE WHAT?

My brother called me at 12:10 a.m. to tell me our father had just taken his last breath. Dad had been living in an extended care facility. My brother was very upset about my father's passing, and then he said, "They want me to get him out of there right away." He asked, "Where am I going to take him?" We thought in a facility where such an event was a regular occurrence they would be prepared to handle the body for a few hours.

HE WAS EXCUSED

At the age of ninety-two, my dad was really not there anymore. He had to wear adult diapers and get help changing them a couple of times a day. I think he could hear but his responses were almost always nasty and obviously confused.

He got a summons to the state grand jury. I tried to explain the situation on the phone but was told he would have to serve.

So about a month before the date he was to report, I sent a letter to the clerk of the jury. I explained they would need someone to change his diaper a few times a day and maybe poke him to keep him awake. And since he cannot walk, what time would the court have someone with a wheel-chair to meet us at the courthouse door and then wheel him around as he might need?

We received a letter within a few days—excused from jury duty.

Was it the dirty diapers or him sleeping in the jury box that convinced them?

BUILDING A NURSING HOME IN MY MOTHER'S HOME

Ten years ago, I came back from Richmond, Virginia, and learned that my mother had been diagnosed with Alzheimer's disease, and I com-mitted to taking care of her at home. The reason I committed to care in her home was because we were told that if you kept your loved one with such a diagnosis in a familiar setting, preferably their home, they did much better. Additionally, my mother had gone straight from college to marriage, to life in a large house with servants, and had no context for communal living. So, I came home and taught myself to care for my mother.

My mother does not quite fit the criteria for Alzheimer's. There are multiple forms of dementia, some caused by brain injury. My mother had been in seven car accidents in her life. It is clear that we could not know the real condition of her brain, the cause of her dementia, or whether the accidents caused damage. It did not matter, she needed care. I had much to learn!

On my caregiver journey, I learned five things: 1) The healthcare industry has no care professionals who can really be trained to take care of individuals with dementia or Alzheimer's disease. The agencies use a pool of people that they pull from. Relying on my skills as a psychologist, I set up a complete training protocol for my mother. I developed a checklist and thought I was doing great, but I found out most agency caregivers don't read it. I had to become the "guru" on developing protocols that the agency caregivers could read. I went through twenty-eight caregivers per year. They would come and not want to do the work. This was my first pain point.

As a clinical psychologist specializing in children and families, I had to teach my mother's agency caregivers about the importance of play in engaging my mother. It was difficult because many of the caregivers were from cultures where they were not taught to play and refused to do so. My mother was an educated person (trained social worker, previous board member, multiple radio appearances) who, despite her dementia, required cognitive stimulation. To this day, I continue to train my mother's caregivers. to go beyond "feeding and wiping" my mother. That appears to be all they are trained to do. It's exhausting. Nobody should have to do this. The agency caregivers push food as a way of engagement, and I stop them because it causes her to gain weight. It breaks your heart.

2) The agency caregivers know nothing about exercise and range of motion. So here I took over; I had to buy many toys and a puzzle. I asked the caregiver whether she could do a puzzle. She replied, "No". I offered to show her. Now, I have to train grown adults who have never learned to play. They know nothing about the body. They take a six-week course as part of their training but cannot

implement a program effectively. They are not evaluated.

I finally employed (paid by me) a physical therapist who has been with my mother for ten years. She supervises them three times per week. I have sheets outlining exercises, many of which can be done in bed. I am engaged 24-7 because the agency caregiver will forget what I am saying by the following week. I work 12-hour days out of the home. On the weekends, I can't leave the caregivers alone with my Mom because they will not do things properly.

3) I found a caregiver with twenty years of experience who I am training to be a care manager. She can replace me so that I can pursue self-care (hairdressing, running errands, taking trips). So this person has done caregiving for twenty years with a friend of mine. I "Uber" her to the house so she can learn to be me and see the person providing care for the weekend. I've learned that I had to have a care manager to supervise. The agency sends different people each weekend, as if a person with dementia can manage multiple caregivers who have to assist her with personal care because she is not mobile.

4) Using the correct tone of voice. The agency

care providers I have experienced shout at my Mom when they want something. When she hears shouting, she becomes terrified. They do not know about voice modulation. I believe this should be added to agency training of care providers along with integrating their cultural norms. I need the agencies to encourage the people doing this work to be interested in enhancing training—to want to have additional training in nursing, nutrition, and the proper way to manage older people's bodies. After doing the training of those who have come to my home for ten years, I am tired.

5) I also want to talk about the amazing support I received from my sororities, the groups I belonged to, and the caregiver support program I started at my church many years ago. I believe it is so important to have family caregivers share with each other. Because my mother's mother had dementia, I tried to get my mother to get a companion before she had difficulties. Still, she resisted, insisting that it would not happen to her. I am developing a mastermind support group focused on developing caregiving planning for the group members. It will enable the members to build upon each member's strengths

and avoid my taking responsibility for all aspects of bringing the plan together.

WHO DO I CALL?

I'll tell you about the most challenging thing because that's the most important thing people need to know. I noticed my mother needed help— she couldn't be left alone in the house because of her behavior. I didn't think it was safe, so she came to live with me.

The most challenging thing was getting help. I mean, I am trying to figure out who to call. Was it eldercare? First, I had a conversation with her doctor. He agreed with me; he did the testing, and he felt she had dementia and it was an early sign of Alzheimer's. He thought she needed help; she needed assistance.

Once that was affirmed, I asked the family, "What will we do?" She needs help; the kids are in college, and I must work. So, I started asking around. I know of people who have people coming to help, but not too many people of color. So, I know people who work for other people. It's pretty prevalent in Caribbean communities for some people to work in someone's home. So, I asked, "How did you get this job?". They replied that they worked for an agency. I asked, "Do I call the agency and say I need someone, and how do they get paid?"

For a while, I couldn't figure it out. Then, I had a conversation with a friend at work, and I told her of the dilemma, and she said, "You have to call managed care." I said, "Who?" I called eldercare, and they said they couldn't help me. I called managed care, and they walked me through the process, which I think many people are unaware of. You have to call managed care, which gets you into the Medicaid office and an in-between office. There was a lot of paperwork. My mother had Medicare, and now she had Medicaid. The managed care office gets you an agency listing, and you choose an agency that gets the aide to come to the house.

It took me a long time to get someone. What I used to have to do was get up early in the morning, prepare her breakfast and lunch, administer her medications and place additional ones on the counter due to her mobility issues, help her with personal care, and then I would run to work. Thank

God I had flexibility at work, and my supervisor understood the situation.

I would call throughout the day to remind her to eat her lunch and to take her medications. Then, after work, I'd run home, and it was time for dinner and more medications, cleaning up, and getting her to bed. Sometimes, this took 'til midnight.

At times, she would scream out my name at night, and I'd run downstairs thinking something was the matter. She might say, "Where did you go? You disappeared!" When I told her I went upstairs to bed, she'd say, "You went upstairs? How come I've never been upstairs?". I look back; it was so frustrating when it happened, but as I recall it, it is like a comedy scene. You really have to go through the experience to understand it. When other people share their experiences with me, I get it immediately. I remember the stage at which I experienced what they were describing.

When we first got the aides, they were unfamiliar with her, her routines, and the house. I still had to wait for them. At first, it was a huge adjustment. If the agency sent one person on Monday, Tuesday, and Wednesday, they would send a different person on Thursday and Friday. I would have to wait to teach each person all the routines, etc. Then they would call you, two to three times during the day, if they were unsure of something.

They would call in the morning to say they were running late, or the agency would call and say, the person you have had can't make it. We're sending you someone else who can't arrive before 11 a.m. You recognize that you cannot leave before they arrive; once they arrive, introducing them to the routines would begin again. You feel like you're a prisoner.

I dealt with that for months until I called managed care and told them I could not deal with it. Get me another agency. I need a stable person. So finally, I got a second agency that consistently provided the same two people. They worked out their schedule. They covered for each other when they had scheduling issues and became like family. I thank God for them.

From the beginning of the caregiving to my mother's passing, it was about five years. You could see the decline during those years. Initially, she would get up and sit at the table to eat. Ultimately, she had difficulty sitting up or walking around, and we had to get her a medical bed. My mother had seven children (one was deceased) and over a dozen grandchildren. She probably only remembered four of us toward the end of her life. She remembered only me after the COVID-19 period because I was always there. My siblings did not come to stay with her. Some would visit for a weekend but not stay beyond that.

She did not want to leave the house when she began to decline. They did not want to come and stay with her if I needed a break or went on vacation. They were busy. Then, if they took her to their homes, the aides would have to travel to their houses, and it became difficult. My daughter would come and stay sometimes.

I was my brother's caregiver, too, due to his heart disease, and he passed a year before my mother. I realized how important it was to have my papers in place. My daughter is a lawyer, so she will know what to do concerning my situation.

Since my Mom passed, I looked back at the situation with joy, and I don't have any resentment. I fear this will happen to me, so I stay active and busy!

IT'S COMPLICATED

I'm doing okay, considering I have to go to a ceremony for my sister's burial on Saturday. And then today, I have my very first court day for my divorce.

I come from a family of seven; six of us are sisters, and one is a brother. My parents separated when I was six years old. My mother moved to the States in the mid-eighties to New York. Then, we followed from Mexico City. We stayed because we fell in love with the system here and the country, and we all stayed with her. My mother worked as a caregiver.

As a matter of fact, she was a maid for a family in Brooklyn. We all came to the state and decided, "No more, she is gonna' stay home, and we'll provide for her." And that's how it went for years and years.

My mother was a very old-fashioned person. She didn't believe much in women's health care. She wasn't sexually active, so she felt that she didn't need to go to have her pap smears and all the annual checkups that she was supposed to. For that reason, when she started having symptoms, it turned out that it was cervical cancer.

When she was diagnosed, we figured, okay, we're gonna do the rounds of chemotherapy, radiation— whatever it takes to save her life. But it didn't turn out that way. She did all of that, and all it did was cause her to suffer because it was pretty advanced. The radiation and chemotherapy were just very aggressive to her body. There was an entire year where six of us sisters were taking turns not to leave my mother alone while she was going back and forth to the hospital. And when the time came that she went home, she was at home with any one of us.

We decided to come and rotate like we did at the hospital. She never really spent one hour without having one of us take care of her. The radiation and the chemotherapy were very, very aggressive. I am sure that a lot of people are treated longer, but for that whole year, she needed so much help that it came to the point that one of us lost our job because we decided to take care of her.

We never had somebody else in the family going through chemo, cancer, or anything like that. So it shook us a bit; it was very brutal. When she passed, we felt the emptiness, the everything that comes with the loneliness. We were overwhelmed during her treatments and so brokenhearted that we never wanted to ask, "Do you have your paperwork ready with whatever properties you have back home in Mexico?"

At that point, we thought it would be cruel to ask, "Where is the money I gave you that you saved for me?" Everything ended up in the air because it never got resolved. Fourteen years later, we are still fixing things with inheritance because it was never resolved.

Three years after my mother's death, I went on a trip to Mexico. Here I am, going to Cancun and having the time of my life. I decided to visit my father in Mexico City because I hadn't seen him for a long time. I went to see him where he lived with his new wife and daughter. When I got there, he was physically shivering, and I knew something was not quite right. My father was terribly ill.

My dad's new wife decided to put him in a low-level hospital. In Mexico, sons and daughters have no say. We all went back to see about my father. First, we had to spend a lot of money to return from New York to Mexico City. We found out about the situation when we arrived in Mexico City.

The wife was the one who made the decisions when my father was there in the hospital. But my father was so ill that my sisters and I decided that we were going to come up with a plan to get him out of that hospital. We wanted to put him in a private hospital where there is dignity and where they have everything to offer a better quality of life.

So that's what we did. We basically kidnapped him. We had to give a little bit of money to the security guards and do those maneuvers. By then, we had already hired an ambulance from a private hospital to transfer him.

In addition to all the fees we had to deal with for the hospital, the airplane tickets, and hotel stays, some of us couldn't even stay together. And the pain that we had to go through, the actual anguish you go through while making decisions. "Okay, so what's the next step?" The meetings with these doctors were difficult. We'd been away from Mexico for so long that when they were using Spanish terminology, it was enough to give us each a heart attack.

The tables were turned from when we arrived in New York. The doctors used these new terms that we hadn't heard in so long, or because we were little, we didn't learn. We never had to go through an illness in a Spanish-speaking hospital.

We had to surrender to the fact that we would pay for his stay. Although my dad had money to be able to cover the cost, when there is a life-or-death situation, and your dad is suffering, you just don't care. You're willing to come up with the fees as long as he will be okay, even though his wife was not cooperating. At one point, we even had a sense that when we found him shivering in his room, we felt that she was waiting for him to die.

It was very scary. We couldn't believe that she dared to leave him in his bed, shivering and unable to move. Of course, he ended up in a better hospital once we saw him in that condition. We went through so much, and after that, my sisters, brothers, and I became really, really close...closer than we ever were.

6

STUBBORNNESS

"Some day you will be old enough to start reading fairy tales again." –C.S. Lewis

TAKING GRANDMA TO THE AIRPORT

GRANDMA WAS RETURNING to Detroit after a weeklong visit with the family. We lived three miles away from JFK and the ride there was fifteen minutes long. This was "back in the day," the nineties, before the major traffic jams and all of the other issues. Grandma's flight was about two hours long and she lived thirty minutes away from the Detroit airport. With check-in (we were at the airport an hour early and there were no outrageous lines), travel, deboarding, bag retrieval, and travel (remember it's "back in the day"), Grandma's time of arrival to her home after dropping her off at JFK was likely to be two hundred fifty minutes (four hours and ten minutes).

We took Grandma to JFK and my mom saw her through the check-in and to her gate. We all got back into the car, my father driving, my mom in the back, and me in the front passenger seat. As we began the trip home, I had no idea what was about to ensue. My father missed the turn for the correct exit from JFK. Uh-oh. My father had reached the point that his poor sense of direction was exacerbated by his refusal to take any suggestions from passengers. So we rode, we rode, and we rode some more! We passed the same landmarks again, and again, and again.

I finally convinced Dad to stop at a gas station, where I exchanged seats with him and drove home. When we finally got home, we checked our messages and Grandma had called multiple times, worried about us not having gotten back home yet. Our fifteen-minute trip had taken over four hours!

WE CAN KEEP GOING!

This happened a few years ago. My dad stopped driving due to age-related issues and my mom had quit driving many years prior. My folks were in their nineties. One day, Dad called me on the phone and said he had a great idea. This is how the conversation went:

With excitement, Dad said, "I have a great idea where you don't need to drive us anymore."

I thought maybe they might call a taxi, so I asked, "What do you plan to do?"

Dad replied, "I will have your mom drive."

I responded, "But Dad, Mom is legally blind." (She had macular degeneration.)

With resolve, Dad answered, "No problem, I will just tell her when to stop, when to go, when to turn."

"But Dad, Mom can't hear anymore," I reminded him.

There was silence on the other end of the phone.

"Oh," was all he could say in response.

7

IMPACT UPON CAREGIVER

"In the end, it's not the years in your life that count. It's the life in your years."
−Often attributed to Abraham Lincoln

THE LONG GOODBYE

HAD HEARD THAT phrase before but I never thought it would relate to my own experience of watching my mother waste away from the ravages of dementia. My mother was seventy-five years old when she was diagnosed with dementia. She lived nine years with this awful disease and during that time my siblings and I had the painful experience of seeing my mother lose the essence of herself.

Before dementia, my mother was a smart, generous, and vibrant woman who centered her life on her children, grandchildren, and great-grandchildren, and a small network of friends. She was also a survivor who possessed enormous strengths at critical times in her life. She lost her mother during early childhood, and shortly afterward she and her grandmother and two sisters joined the northern migration to arrive in New York City for a better life. She became a mother at fifteen years of age and at the age of thirty-four she becomes a widow after the untimely death of her husband.

My father's death left my mother with the sole responsibility of caring for four children alone without a high school diploma and no work experience; she had been a homemaker all her adult life. This crisis mobilized her to embark upon an educational and career trajectory to attain her GED and a stable job as a practical nurse. She retired from nursing at sixty-five and lived a pretty comfortable life until she was diagnosed with dementia.

Despite being diagnosed at seventy-five, in hindsight my mother was showing early signs of cognitive decline at least two years before, but we were either in denial or didn't really understand what was happening to her. In retrospect, we noticed odd behavior, like the time she showed up at my daughter's wedding with a paper party bag she was using as a purse.

Then she began to exhibit irrational beliefs about imminent harm to others—but nothing that was harmful to her. For example, I had planned to go on a cruise and upon hearing about this, my mother became fixated on the belief that I would fall overboard, drown, and she would never see me again.

Her behaviors became more serious, like the time I had been trying to call her for two days without reaching her. This prompted me to call the concierge in her building to ask him to check on her. He did and told me she was fine but when he asked her why she had not answered his call before he knocked on the door, she told him she lost her phone. Later that day, my brother went to visit her to find that the landline phone was disconnected and stuffed in her handbag. When he asked her why, she responded that she liked to keep her phone in her bag when she went to the store.

During my morning calls she began to tell me she couldn't talk to me during this time anymore because she was visiting with three ladies in her apartment. After not getting any clear answer about who these women were, I showed up one morning only for her to tell me she was talking about the women on *The View*, who she believed were talking to her through her television set.

Finally, two things occurred that became the tipping point for us to decide our mother could not be left alone. Her management office called to inform me that my mother had not paid her rent in three months, which was unusual because my mother had paid her rent on time for the past twenty-five years.

Next, the concierge called me at midnight to inform me this was the second time our mother tried to leave the building in the middle of the winter wearing just her bathrobe and pajamas. During this incident, she became very agitated when they tried to stop her so they called me to ask if one of us could come over immediately to intervene because otherwise they would have no recourse but to call 911 for help. Luckily, my sister was on duty at Metropolitan Hospital and left immediately to accompany my mother upstairs to her apartment.

It was determined that I would begin the process of getting our mother evaluated and I started with the primary care provider who had been treating her for several years. After examining my mother and administering a brief diagnostic screening that she failed, he privately recommended that I get her evaluated at Mount Sinai's Alzheimer's Disease Research Center. I followed up and accompanied my mother to a series of evaluations and diagnostic tests that resulted in a definitive diagnosis of dementia.

Since there is no cure for dementia and my mother had no serious medical conditions, the treatment recommendation was a prescription for donepezil (Aricept) to slow down the progression of the disease, keeping her safe and monitored at all times, accessing home care, and finding a day program to provide her with stimulation.

My three siblings and I became our mother's caregivers and at the time we ranged in age from fifty-nine to sixty-one. We had very full lives; my sister and I were married with adult children and grandchildren and we all had full-time jobs. There were no other family or friends to help us. We also decided we wanted to keep our mother in her own apartment and surrounded by the things that were important to her.

The positive thing that resulted from our mother's diagnosis of dementia is that it brought my siblings and me closer together. We agreed about her care and all end-of-life decisions, financial responsibility for her care was shared equally, and we took turns caring for her on the weekends until she passed away.

It is important to note here that since my mother worked, received a pension and Social Security benefits, and had insurance, her income precluded her from getting affordable home-care services. In fact, when I inquired about out-of-pocket costs, the fees were cost-prohibitive and many of the home-care companies didn't even get back to me when they learned my mother did not have Medicaid. So in addition to managing the financial costs of maintaining her living expenses, we were also responsible for paying for home care services, which became another expense added to our own living expenses.

Immediately following the diagnosis, we hired a woman through word of mouth to work from 8:00 a.m. to 6:00 p.m. Monday through Saturday. Then my sister developed a schedule of weekly evening and weekend coverage among the four of us to ensure our mother would never be left alone. This plan lasted a couple of months but it was not sustainable. We realized we actually needed live-in care.

Luckily, one of the nurses my sister worked with had a sister-in-law who had just ended her home-care assignment and was free to take on another private client. I met her and checked references and hired her to work as a live-in home attendant. She worked full-time with my mother for five years until she could no longer physically take care of her alone.

Toward the end stages of my mother's bout with dementia, she became totally dependent and unable to do anything for herself. She required comprehensive care because she was unable to walk and she needed to be lifted in and out of bed and the bathtub and transported to a wheelchair and a therapeutic chair daily. We knew we needed extra care but were challenged with how to pay for it during this time, when we began to pay attention to her baseline functioning.

Whenever we saw that she was functioning below her baseline, we determined, and accurately so, that she was suffering from an acute medical condition. This resulted in our use of ER services and brief hospitalizations that were very disruptive to us and her caregivers.

It was during this time that she was diagnosed with recurring UTIs, which are common and quite serious in elderly women diagnosed with dementia. During the third hospitalization, a nurse practitioner approached me and informed me about hospice care that my mother would be eligible for. She explained its benefits, which would prevent unnecessary and disruptive hospitalizations, because the service comes with a nurse practitioner who makes weekly home visits and would be equipped to monitor and treat any medical issues my mother experienced. In addition, the service comes with family support and counseling, chaplain services, and support for end-of-life care.

It is important to access important resources: family, home care, Alzheimer's organizations, elder care lawyers, group support, and hospice care.

I had learned about and attended a free seminar the Alzheimer's Association offered on the importance of accessing the services of an elder care lawyer. While there, I learned about the legal services that were helpful in securing Medicaid for home care services. This information was invaluable to me and my siblings in accessing Medicaid for our mother. This enabled us to contract with a home-care company that assigned us a home health aide. She turned out to be a skilled and compassionate person who remained with our family until my mother passed away. Both home-care attendants became integral members of our family, and we remain in contact with them today.

Coincidentally, on the day I attended the elder care seminar, participants were offered an opportunity to attend a group for daughters of mothers with Alzheimer's. I attended, and as group members began to talk about the grief they were experiencing, my floodgates began to open and I could not stop crying. I knew I felt overwhelmed, was extremely sad, and experienced a lot of anxiety that manifested in sleep problems—but hearing others express their experiences with those same struggles and attaching the term "anticipatory grief" to what we were all going through was very meaningful to me.

I experienced anticipatory grief for nine years. I mourned the mother I knew and had a relationship with before she was diagnosed with Alzheimer's and during the nine years she and I lived with her dementia. I held on to the beginning phases of her dementia when, despite her cognitive decline, she was able to express her awareness of her need for help and she seemed to be aware of how we were affected.

Two of these times stand out for me. The first occurred when my sister and I were in the bank to file our power of attorney document and I over-heard my mother telling my sister that she didn't know why she couldn't fill out her checks anymore, and she felt bad about her children having to care for her. My sister stated, "Don't worry Mom; we got you. We love you."

The second happened one day when I was feeding her because she suddenly lost the ability to feed herself. She noticed my tears and turned to me and said, "Honey, stop crying for me. I'll be okay."

The grief I continued to experience occurred during the progression of each phase of my mother's dementia until she reached the end stage of her life, indicated by her inability to take in water or food. Hospice services offered choices of how we wanted to manage this phase of our mother's care. We decided, as per our advanced health care directive, that we would allow our mother to make her transition within her home, being surrounded by her family who loved her and the things she loved and cherished.

Finally, I believe the anticipatory grief I experienced during my long goodbye was felt much more intensely and emotionally than the grief I experienced upon my mother's final death. I miss her immensely and am saddened by her not being in my life. My grief is felt in waves and at special times of the year, like on Mother's Day, our shared birthdays in December, holidays, and the many different milestones she will miss. However, I am very comforted in knowing that my siblings and I were able to take care of her with love and compassion, just as she took care of us.

THE TREE APPEARED FROM NOWHERE

There were three of us in the car. I was driving. Mom was in the back. As I drove down the long driveway, Mom began to fuss. I can't even remember what. Suddenly, out of nowhere, a tree appeared and I, who had no history of accidents, ran into it. No real damage though my nerves were on edge and the fussing made it worse.

It was time for a reset. Leaving both parties in the car, I went back inside the house for half an hour. I came back to the car, resumed driving, and successfully navigated the long driveway.

PERHAPS THEY LOST MY MOTHER

My mom developed dementia after my father died. She ultimately resided at a nursing home and used a wheelchair. One day, at the time her medication was to be administered, Mom was nowhere to be found. They called me at work as I visited daily. I was "fit to be tied." How had she escaped her room in a wheelchair? What had happened to her?

After a several-hour search, she was located asleep in bed with another resident who she mistook for my father. The nursing home staff helped her out of the room, during which time, Mom asked, "Why are you taking me out of my bedroom?" I was so embarrassed but eventually the humor of the situation settled in, and now this story makes me smile.

ELEVEN ELEVEN

I was my mom's primary caregiver. Toward the end, that included sucking smoke up into a water pipe for her so she could quickly inhale some high-grade medical marijuana. She became too weak to hold the pipe for more than a second so I would prep it for her.

"Could you use a puff?" I'd ask.

In desperation, she would shout yes every time. She needed it for the nausea and the pain of spinal stenosis, and I needed it just as badly as she did. We became too thin together, as fight-or-flight hijacked our bodies.

When she was finally prescribed morphine, a friend who had been given some after surgery told us Mom would be having some wonderful dreams. We couldn't wait. After a week, my mom admitted to me it really didn't do much for the pain. However, it did cause some life-changing hallucinations.

At first, when she would ask me questions about things I couldn't see or hear, I was at a loss. My mom had drilled into me that she would never forgive me if I lied to her, and I knew she meant it. She also had a form saying that she would sue you for assault if you took her to the hospital, even if she was unconscious. So in the beginning I would try to make my voice soft and say, "The morphine is making you hallucinate."

"That's a very rude thing to say to someone," she pointed out.

My cousin, Kate, modeled some creative responses. When she found my mother in her walk-in closet in the middle of the night, she asked her, "What are you looking for?"

My mom said, "The baby."

Without missing a beat, Kate told her, "Oh, the baby's in the bed," and my mom went back to bed like a lamb.

Sometimes I didn't have to answer her questions because instead of waiting for a response, she would keep talking. Like, "Did you see the *size* of those flames?"

I just looked at her. She didn't miss a beat. "I'm going to have to go *through* those flames!" she told me.

I shook my head. Her plan was to be cremated—was she getting a preview? "What are we going to do?" she finally asked me. "How are we going to communicate once I've crossed over?" I hadn't figured this one out yet but out of thin air came the perfect answer: 11:11.

I don't know how many years my mom and I shared a ritual that involved *happening* to catch sight of the time at 11:11. We liked the idea of praying five times a day and decided to use 11:11 as a time when we would shout, "Eleven eleven" and immerse ourselves in silent gratitude for the remainder of that minute.

This answer satisfied my mom, and I know when I catch sight of it that she is waving hello. Our water bill, which I finally paid months after she had left her body, came out to $1,111. I explained at her service how 11:11 was going to function as a portal, and now I'm telling you. So please, feel free to join us anytime if you happen to catch it.

THE GHOST

I work as a caregiver in a memory care facility, and I have many fond memories and stories of various residents. But one stands out.

One day I was asked to work the first half of the night shift. Weird things happen at all hours in a memory care facility but the night shift has long quiet times that make it very eerie between room checks.

On this night, I was walking out of the kitchen after finishing up a few chores. I almost ran headfirst into one of our wanderers. She looked pale, gaunt, and a bit haphazard because it was midnight and she had been in bed for hours. The white gauzy nightgown she was wearing really added to the effect.

I jumped out of my skin first. After taking a few deep breaths, I said, "Well hello (resident name). What can I do for you?"

Now usually this woman can't speak or understand cues and is not aware of her surroundings. She's pretty far down the rabbit hole. But I talked to her anyway because it's a natural part of interaction and the sound of a sweet voice talking to her usually calmed her down.

But this time, she looked me square in the eye with a deadly serious face and said, "Cookies."

We had milk and cookies and laughed our asses off at late-night *Futurama* reruns. She was lucid for about two hours.

I never saw her come out of herself like that again. But she was always very sweet to me, patting my arm, following me around, and such.

She passed this last spring, and I was lucky enough to get invited to her memorial.

Rest in peace, my lady. I miss you terribly.

SHE LOVED HORSES

My wife *loves* horses. She grew up around them, volunteered at stables, and took some riding lessons.

Fast-forward thirty years and she's wheelchair-bound and at a parade. A couple of officers are nearby, keeping an eye on things. As she worked her way over, she asked if she could pet the horse; the officer said yes and she was able to place her hand on the horse's nose and stroke the side of my face.

We both "ugly cried" like crazy afterward. I'll never forget that moment.

Another memorable moment included taking the kids back to school after she came back home from the hospital. We lived close enough that the power wheelchair made it to school. She got to have a long hug with the youngest before the little guy walked in for his first day of school.

THE DILEMMA

When I was a young child, my mother made certain I received the best education and guidance about life. Though we lived in the projects, she made sure I was "in them but not of them." She enrolled me in every extracurricular program available. When I was about thirteen or fourteen years old, my mom became addicted to crack. Though she still pushed education, we grew apart. I was able to go to my aunts' homes when things became too difficult at home.

I went away to college and never returned home. As a defense mechanism, I did every program available to university students. What cemented my not returning to my mother's home was seeing her on one attempted visit and not recognizing her. When I returned to my hometown, I would stay with friends who lived near her or I would stay with my grandmother or aunts.

After I graduated from college, my mother began to have medical crises: heart failure, the need for a pacemaker, and a stroke. She is also legally blind. Her siblings' health began to fail and one of them passed away.

I was drawn back into the situation. My mother was put out of her apartment and I was able to get her into a senior-citizen apartment. I was able to find a person who provides care Monday through Friday for her.

In the interim, my career took off and I am in a high-level position. I am married with two children, one of whom has special needs, but I go to take care of my mother on Sundays.

I buy all of her groceries. I supplement her income to enable her to pay for the cost of her apartment. At first, I resented it and I was angry. Now I go through good and bad days. On top of this, my father, with whom I have had no contact, has begun to reach out to me. I feel so overwhelmed.

STAGES OF CARE

Sometimes caregivers can go a long time with very little to smile about. Getting services for my mother fell into five distinct phases.

Phase One: My mother was diagnosed with sarcoidosis, which affected her lungs for some period of time. Soon after, she was diagnosed with cancer and began chemotherapy. While she was in the chemotherapy phase of treatment, she had a stroke.

She was admitted to the intensive care unit of the hospital. As an only child, I needed to be there all day; therefore I took leave from work. I went home at night, concerned because she woke up and did not know where she was. This made me feel terrible but I could not stay at the hospital twenty-four hours a day.

Phase Two: Mom was referred to a rehabilitation center, where she stayed for one month. It immediately became clear that she would need help with daily living skills, including toileting. I again stayed all day. The nursing staff was only too happy to have me assist my mother with her needs. I watched as her roommate rang for assistance and noted the more than thirty minutes it took for someone to come. I started ringing my mother's bell when her roommate needed help. I was becoming exhausted.

Phase Three: My mother was referred to a nursing home, this time for three months. There, she began receiving physical therapy in the morning and occupational therapy in the afternoon. I was on call for her, and any time the phone rang my nerves were jangled.

I went to visit her seven days a week. They would not allow me to spend the night. On occasion, I had to talk her through coughing spasms over the telephone. After they realized I continued to sit outside of her group physical therapy session every morning, they allowed me to come into the room, which made it more fun for all involved. After one month, she was walking with a walker. I would "break her out" to see other doctors who were not associated with the nursing facility.

Phase Four: She was sent home and had attendant services three times a week and physical therapy two times per week. I had been on leave from work but finally had to return. I engaged the attendant to work an additional two days. When I came home, the attendant left—and I had no other assistance. Family members came, supposedly to help, but the result was that I was cooking for them too. I did engage a driver to take us to my mother's medical appointments at this point.

Phase Five: Mom began to have seizures, was sent to ICU, and then to hospice. For the first time since my mother was diagnosed with cancer, I was able to exhale. The facility was actually comfortable, the staff was gentle and supportive of my mother and me, and pain management was provided.

In February 2012, my mom was diagnosed with Alzheimer's disease. In May 2012, my father died suddenly without any warning. My mom lived in New Jersey, and I live in Manhattan, New York. In June 2012, I was diagnosed with cancer. In July 2012, I was diagnosed with another unrelated cancer of the thyroid that affected my vocal cords. I was juggling a lot of balls at that time.

By the fall of 2012, I'd had three surgeries and chemotherapy, and was taking care of my mom. I would have moved my mom to a facility earlier but honestly, it was taking so long for me to heal that I couldn't. The thyroid tumor was connected to a vocal cord so in addition to removing my thyroid, they had to remove a part of my vocal cord and I had to learn how to talk again. I kept telling myself you can't ruin a bad time.

I finally got her into a facility in February 2013 in Manhattan, just fifteen blocks from my house so I can see her more easily. When she was in New Jersey, I was traveling to her at least five days a week just to make sure everything was taken care of.

My parents had a housekeeper who I hired to go and be with my mother when she wasn't working another job. Eventually, I had to take the car keys away from my mother because it was no longer safe for her to drive.

The first time I took my mom to the bank, I learned she could not fill out a bank withdrawal form. Though my mother had worked as an English teacher, my father took care of everything with respect to their business affairs. It was at that moment that the magnitude of everything that lay before me became real.

Since I was not an only child, some assistance would have been helpful. My brother was dismissive of the situation. He has a wife and two children but they just did nothing. The only time they helped was during Hurricane Sandy. I could not get from Manhattan to my mom. I found out she was in the house with no electricity. I told them to go and get her. They did so and they also took all of her jewelry. It was the last time I asked for help and the last time they provided any.

It became apparent my mother was not going to be able to care for herself, so I jumped right in. This was not easy because I was running my own business. I felt utterly and thoroughly overwhelmed. I was extremely depressed. I didn't go anywhere or do anything except care for Mom and go to work. There was just more stuff that kept piling on and on.

There wasn't anybody to reach out to on a regular basis. I had a friend who would periodically just go and pick up my mom and take her out, but I have a very difficult time asking anyone for help. When I did ask my brother, there was always some reason it couldn't be done so I just stopped asking. He once said he knew I wanted to do everything myself. Honestly, it was just easier to go and do it than to worry about whether someone was going to do it. I just didn't have the time to go back and forth. I promised myself I would not lose my sense of humor.

When Mom was admitted to a nursing home, I went every day until one day she said, "Oh, you're here again!" I was elated; I could cut back. Then the pandemic came, and I could not visit.

Once the pandemic "lockdown" ended, we were assigned a day and time I could visit my mom. She was mostly nonverbal for six years but I became used to nonverbal cues. She doesn't take her eyes off me when I'm there. I feed her as she cannot feed herself.

Three years ago this July, she was diagnosed with

uterine cancer and eventually entered hospice care. She stopped going downhill so I received a phone call saying she didn't meet the hospice requirements anymore.

My mom suffered from migraine headaches her whole life; she went to a variety of doctors to treat them. She was on so much medication before she was admitted to the nursing home, she had developed a tremor in her hand. Within one week, she was off the medication, and they handed me a small plastic zip bag of medication. She's now working with an art therapist and producing a lot of colorful artwork. The lines in the artwork reflect the fact that the tremor is gone.

I'm starting to feel like I deserve a life for myself. I feel I have been given the opportunity to walk my mother to her graduation and through the stories I am telling, I want to help others who are dealing with similar issues as the primary caregiver.

IT'S THE LITTLE THINGS

I have had three people tell me I am doing a good job taking care of my elder. One was a visiting nurse and I think she was being nice, but it was kind of her to take the time in her busy day to say that. A hairdresser cutting his hair said, "I can tell you take good care of him; he is shaved and his skin is clean behind the ears." It was really unexpected how good that made me feel.

And then a podiatrist, when they took his socks off, said, "Well someone has been taking care of these feet." As pathetic as it sounds, I really cling to those kind words. Every night when I am putting on new socks and doing the tedious moisturizer routine, their words ring in my ears and put wind in my sails.

OF COURSE

My mom has Alzheimer's disease. A few weeks ago, she sent me an email asking me to pick up a cake for my brother's birthday the next day, and that she would be making his favorite dinner.

She's long past being able to prepare food, and my brother's birthday isn't for months.

I just found it so heartwarming and sweet that the knowledge she holds on to the tightest, while everything else slips away, is taking care of her boys.

Of course, we went ahead and had the dinner, cake, and party the next day. How could we not?

KEEPING TRACK

My eighty-six-year-old mom with stage five/six dementia lives with me. She not only gets confused all the time about where she is, but she also thinks I have more than one home. Once I tried to tell her that I'm single, I can only afford one mortgage, and I can barely afford it at that.

She replied, "You know, if you sold that other house, you could probably just pay this house off. Did you ever think of that?"

I gave up at that point and said, "Okay, can you point this house out to me? As soon as I find out where this house is I'm gonna sell it."

She looked at me for a few moments and then said in her wisest voice, "I think you need to keep better track of your houses. That's your main problem right there."

Thanks, Mom, you're right. I need to keep better track of my houses. Story of my life.

CAREGIVING THROUGH THE AGES

My mother suffered from severe lung disease all her life. When she was eight or so, she developed pneumonia. Without antibiotics (they were developed after WWII), her lungs never cleared from the original infection, even when antibiotics were available. Her doctor cautioned her about having another child after my sister was born. My mother got pregnant, and both of us survived, but it took an enormous additional toll on her lungs to have me.

For all of my life, I have had eczema, and as a child, I scratched in my sleep. My mother would wake me up to tell me to stop scratching. Then I listened to her cough and hack from her bedroom and wondered if I would be the one to hear her take her last breath. My father had died when I was two, so she was a single parent.

In high school, my two older sisters had moved out, so I was the one she counted on. She basically took care of herself, and as soon as I got my license, my job was shopping, taking her where she needed to go, and doing whatever she wanted me to do.

I left for college in 1967, and she was alone, depending on some social services, but they were minimal at the time. Shortly after I graduated, she had gotten to the point of needing oxygen full-time. She had moved into a senior housing complex and had an oxygen generator with a long cord to which she was basically tethered.

In 1982, she had gotten to the point where she needed more help. My sisters and I discussed options, which were very limited, but the one that seemed the best was moving her to a lung specialty hospital in the next town. It had been a county tuberculosis (TB) hospital and had been repurposed for other lung diseases. It looked more like an asylum than a hospital.

It was horrible. My mother was in a ward with about ten patients on either side of a large room. Each patient had a cubicle with a bed, side table, chair, and commode. Each cubicle was separated by a flimsy wall about six feet high with no top and a curtain entrance. Since all the patients were there because of lung disease, breathless coughing, and hacking were constant.

To this day, I still feel guilty that we talked her into going there, where she stayed for a year and a half until she died. However, I still can't think of anything else we could have done. She wanted to see me every weekend, and with few exceptions, I drove ninety miles each way to see her every Saturday.

In about 1981, my mother-in-law had surgery for cancer in her spine. Her vertebrae had to be broken to get at the cancer. A second surgery was for rods to be inserted to stabilize the spine and a third one to "adjust the rods,' none of which helped her mobility and all of which ended in constant debilitating pain. She, too, lived alone, and I was the go-between for her medical issues whenever possible.

She was very independent and tried her hardest to keep any bad things from me and her son. Since she was not mobile, she had help from senior services—meals-on-wheels, visiting nurses, and even home doctor visits. She never complained, but it was obvious that she was in constant pain, though she didn't act like it. We were very good friends and talked a lot about life and death, and she made her wishes known to me and from me to her son. The one thing she allowed me to do was help her with a weekly shower and re-bandaging her back, but I checked in frequently as she lived nearby.

Possibly the same year, my sister, who lived in the next town, was diagnosed with breast cancer. She had two little kids, aged three and five, and her husband was not much help. I took her to doctors in Boston when I could and when she couldn't get others to accompany her. After treatments, she was clear, but at almost the exact five-year point, she was diagnosed with a different type of breast cancer in the other breast and had all the treatments for that. I didn't do much except for trips to Boston and trying to keep track of what was happening with her.

At that time, three people close to me had very serious illnesses at the same time. My mother died in 1984, and two years later, my husband had a heart attack, so then I was back to three of the closest people in my life.

My sister continued her battle with cancer that developed into leukemia from the radiation from her first treatments. In about 1991 or 92, she needed a bone marrow transplant, and I was a match. A year later, my mother-in-law died, and my sister was in a clinical trial where my blood was needed. All of her struggles ended in 1994.

I only had my husband to worry about, and for five years, things were calm. We concentrated on ourselves and enjoyed life. Then he developed an infection in his foot that would not heal, and his leg had to be amputated. After many hospitalizations, they sent him home to die. At that point, I was the caregiver for about two months. He wasn't talking about his feelings, so I didn't either. I figured it was his journey, and I had to ensure he could do it his way. It all ended in 2000 when he died.

My job was stressful by itself, and worrying and thinking about the sick people took extra energy. I was a big person before all this, but I got progressively larger with each passing year. Even after everyone was gone, my weight ballooned, and in 2008, I had gastric bypass surgery. I lost a lot of weight initially, but six weeks after surgery, I was cleared for exercise. The second time I went rowing in my boat, I had a heart attack while rowing, my favorite activity. I am okay, on meds, but heavy again.

And so, it goes. Certainly not the story of folks who are actual caregivers, but when on the periphery, it still took a toll because those folks were always on my mind. I don't consider what little I did as anything special. It was just what you do for loved ones when the situation calls for it.

SHE WAS MY "RIDE OR DIE"

I'll probably talk in more general terms about caring for my mother. I took care of my mother for fifteen years. My story is a little strange. I moved home after my father passed away in 1999, and my mother was sixty-eight at the time. Though I had not lived with her up until that time, I had started to take on some of the caregiving roles—making sure the house was clean or a cleaning woman was coming, making sure the car was serviced, making sure the groceries were bought, making sure things were taken care of in the home. If something broke, I repurchased it.

In 2006, she was seventy-five, and I had my Mom move in with me because she was starting to have more problems. She retired from work at seventy-four. Both of my parents were pharmacists. I knew I was moving to California. The winters were getting harder, and I was more concerned about ice and stuff and the possibility of her falling. I didn't feel that Chicago was the safest place for her to be alone.

So, then we moved to California in 2009. I took care of her from 2006 to when she passed away in 2020. I was very lucky that my mother was very, very healthy up until she passed away at eighty-nine. She very rarely went to the doctor, no medications.

She fractured her hip in 1997 and had a pin put in, and then she fractured it again because you know that happens. She had to have a hip replacement; it was after my dad passed, so it was 2000 or 2001. And so, I was already doing stuff then. Like leaving my work early to go to the rehabilitation facility to make sure her physical therapy was happening because she didn't want to do it. I was like, listen, stats are against you. Only one-third of people with a hip fracture end up walking and living independently. It's bad. But, even with her hip fracture, she didn't use any aids to walk around. She didn't need glasses if you can imagine.

She was overall very healthy, but, as you know, as people get older, it becomes more challenging. You have to watch their safety; they like doing things they shouldn't. She fractured her elbow because she got on a stepping stool to water a plant, even though the cleaning people were there. I had to fly home from Phoenix, and then I was like, I need to rethink how I'm doing this because my mother "writes checks her body can't cash."

I moved from San Diego to LA to be closer to my brother so that if I wasn't there, he could help, which was good. Sometimes, when you are not with a person all the time and they say, "Oh, that's okay," and my brother would say okay, I'd have to step in and say, "No, no, no, no. That's not how it works." And she had other health scares and hospitalizations.

Her doctor didn't know how her potassium got so low for one of these. Basically, she "wolverined" like she just adapted to the low potassium, and it was critically low because it hurt her back. She didn't want to eat, and I was my mother, about 125 lbs. soaking wet and 4 foot 10 inches tall. It wasn't like other catastrophic occurrences with caregiving; it was these "itty-bitty" daily trying to keep her on this razor-edged line of health issues.

At one point, I stopped traveling for about a month so that I was home every day to ensure she was eating and walking. And I was also running a company, and you can't share that with your clients. They don't care about your personal life. They just want the work done. It was about handling things in a way that my clients had no idea what was going on in my personal life; I worked from the hospital when my Mom's potassium was low.

I used to tell her, "You paid all that money for Medicare, so you should take advantage and eat a sandwich." My mother was always concerned about spending too much money. She'd check her Medicare bill and identify discrepancies. But my clients didn't know I was taking calls from a hospital. I was doing work from her room. I would keep her company, and she had a potassium drip. There was a lot of that.

But I did not want people to say, "You have all this competing responsibility, so you won't have time for me." Interestingly, they don't say that about people who have children. I got that from family members who totally diminished what I was doing. I didn't get married. I didn't have children because this was my "charge."

I have one sister and one brother. I was lucky that my mother was so healthy and was very open to experiences. She was my "ride or die." She would travel with me. She was very adaptable. I don't think my sister and brother understand, even to this day, the level of responsibility that I took that not only meant they didn't have to deal with, but they didn't have to find someone to care for her because I was it. Cleaner, chauffeur, appointment maker, chef, companion.

During the COVID-19 pandemic, I was a basket case because I had to go out, and I was like, "I could give it to her." The COVID-19 vaccine wasn't available until later, and my mother passed away before that. But I believe even if she were alive, I would have been the one to get sick because she never got sick.

During that time, my business doubled because I was known as "the fixer," and my clients came to me to help with leads. I had a ton of work on top of going to the grocery store at 6 a.m. with gloves and disinfectant. My mother questioned why I was doing all of this. I explained that I had to protect her and me from getting ill. I asked, "What would happen if I got sick and couldn't care for you? As it turned out, I broke my elbow at one point, and neighbors helped by bringing in food and stuff.

Ultimately, my mother had a heart attack. The doctors thought she might survive it. She had the attack on the morning of October 5. She was joking with the ambulance driver. She went to the emergency room and then the ICU. We thought she was going to pass away then, but she rallied. The evening came, and she was sitting up in bed. She complained she was tired. The next morning, she passed away. There was no long illness or prolonged hospital stay.

ACKNOWLEDGMENTS

THANK YOU TO everyone who contributed to this effort! Your generosity helps to move caregiving to the "front burner" so more of us are "seen" and hopefully cared for and about!

Allyson Straker-Banks, PhD

(In Memoriam) Dolores Y. Straker, PhD

Robert Freeman, MD

Aisha Parillon, MSW

Ruth C. Browne, SD

Sandra C. Chapman, MPA, educator and former Brooklyn deputy borough president

Patricia Bryant-Reid, LCSWR

Christine Rudisel, PhD, associate professor

Linda Hurwitz, MA, exit strategy consultant

Cheryl N. Williams, MA, former university associate dean of special programs, The City University of New York

Rich Buyer

Cary Hamilton, LCSW, RPT, Clinical Supervisor, The Hamilton Practice

Elizabeth "Dr. E" Carter, PhD, CEO, corporate elevation strategist

Dolores Swirin-Yao, MA

Jacqueline McMickens, Esq.

Ummulkhair Muhammed, MA, MS

Linda Rhodes Jones

Phyllis Stubbs, MD

Sara Bilik

Sondra E. Buesing Riley

Judith Acosta

Diane Nathaniel

Ed Knox, PhD

Sonia Banks, PhD

Reverend Linda Jackson

Judith Benjamin

Sondra E. Buesing Riley

Sandy MacFarlane

Lisa Apolinski, CMC, Founder of 3 Dog Write

Nigel W. Gretton

Edeline Mitton, MEd, MPH

Florencia Juarez, Hygienist

Reddit Usernames:

Katiekate
freqflyer
AvalonBane
Metallic-Blue
Pacersfan1956
gizmo78
12littlepaws
bbooks5720
SeniorStruggles
lizzy1952

WORKS CITED

1. "New Study Reveals Number Of Unpaid Caregivers In America Grew By 9.5 Million In Five Years To Total 53 Million," AARP.org, May 14, 2020, https://press.aarp.org/2020-5-14-Caregiving-in-the-US-Report.
2. In reference to Samuel Taylor Coleridge's poem, "The Rime of the Ancyent Marinere," 1798.

ENDNOTES

1. In Abigail Pesta, "Michelle Obama Keeps It Real," *Marie Claire*, July 18, 2021, https://www.Marie Claire.com/politics/news/a2132/Michelle-Obama-interior-media/.
2. In "Tina Turner: The Shocking Story Of A Battered Wife Who Escaped To Fame And Fortune," *Ebony,* November 1986, 41.

ABOUT THE CAREGIVER AND EDITOR

Recognized as one of the most prominent voices for caregiver advocacy, Pamela Straker, PhD (Dr. Pam) is an award-winning keynoter, bestselling author, and leading authority on mental health and wellness.

Leveraging over twenty years as a caregiver and thirty years of experience as a practicing psychologist, Dr. Pam impacts audiences with her mission to normalize and destigmatize mental health conversations. She trains individuals, corporations, and organizations worldwide on how to have greater clarity, awareness, a new way of thinking, and a sustainable plan for assuming the role of a caregiver.

Dr. Pam speaks on the topic of heroic caregiving to give caregivers a voice and a context in which they can find balance while they appreciate themselves, the many complexities they manage, and their right and responsibility to seek happiness even when caring for others. Caregivers are offered a process through which they can address the daily, ongoing minor and major crises.

Dr. Pamela Straker

Leadership Speaker & Coach

Author of **Heroic Caregiver**,
An Anthology of Lessons on Resilience, Coping, and Laughter

Pamela D. Straker, PhD has been a caregiver for members of her family for more than 20 years and has written a book on the topic. Dr. Straker (Dr. Pam) is a licensed psychologist with more than 30 years of experience and is committed to speaking, encouraging, and providing insight to leaders and caregivers.

SIGNATURE TOPICS

✓ Leading, Caring, & Balancing it all
✓ Pivotal Moments in Heroic Caregiving
✓ Using Stories To Convey Caregiver Heroics
✓ Developing a "Caregiver Legacy Plan"
✓ Protecting your team: How to lead those who give care

EMAIL
DrPam@heroiccaregiver.com

WEBSITE
drpamstaker.com

PHONE
917-693-6263

"Pam is an engaging professional whose wealth of knowledge and experience as a Caregiver make the resources that she shares very relatable."
Aisha Parillon, LMSW, Health Advocate

June 12th

Made in the USA
Middletown, DE
18 March 2025

72848496R00102